Buzzworthy

How to Use This Book

Each biography in this book is paired with a cocktail recipe. Some recipes contain smaller sub-recipes for syrups or infused alcohols; you can find these at the back of the book, in a section called Recipes.

Uncertain about a piece of equipment, a type of glass, a garnish, or a particular ingredient? You can find descriptions of all of these things at the front of the book, in sections called Basic Equipment, Glassware, Cocktail Ingredients, Types of Alcohol, Cocktails for Dietary Restrictions, and Garnishes and Rims.

The following measurements and abbreviations also appear throughout the book:

1 shot = 1 oz / 30 ml

*   Denotes low proof (lower alcohol than a typical cocktail, about 4–7%)

**   Denotes zero-proof (a cocktail with no alcohol)

And finally, if you want to explore the writing of the women in *Buzzworthy*, there's a TBR List at the back featuring selected books and essays—keep it handy for when you hit up your local bookstore or library.

Basic Equipment

You'll need a few tools in order to properly assemble a cocktail.

Shaker
There are different varieties of shaker. The easiest one to use is the standard shaker, which features three parts: a bottom, a built-in strainer, and a cap. Another option is a Boston shaker, which has two roughly equal-sized parts: a metal bottom and a glass (or metal) top. If you use one of these you'll also need to buy a strainer, since they don't have one built in. Boston shakers are popular with professional bartenders because they're unfussy and easy to clean, and you'll find they work best if you want to make multiple cocktails.

Strainer
You'll need one of these if you use a Boston shaker. There are different types: a Hawthorne strainer is a steel paddle that fits over the end of your Boston shaker and does the trick for most drinks, while a fine strainer is used for drinks like Martinis, where you don't want little pieces of ice or citrus to ruin the smooth surface of the drink.

Jigger / shot glass
A jigger or shot glass is used for measuring alcohol or other liquids for cocktails. They come in different sizes, most typically 1 to 2 oz / 30 to 60 ml (although you can find them smaller and larger).

Mixing glass
Not all cocktails are shaken. For those that are stirred, you'll need a mixing glass. You can buy one specifically made for the job, but you can also just use a pint glass.

Bar spoon
A long, slender spoon that can be used to mix stirred drinks, a bar spoon is also sometimes used as a measure; it's equal to 1 teaspoon.

Muddler
A muddler is a tool used to mash fruits or herbs at the bottom of a drink. Muddlers can be made from wood or metal, though the metal varieties tend to last longer.

Citrus squeezer

You don't need a high-end juicer to squeeze citrus
fruits. There are different types, but the easiest
is the hand-held press, which allows you to squeeze
a lemon or lime one half at a time.

Blender

If you want to make blended drinks, you'll need a
blender. It doesn't need to be expensive or high-end,
but you do need one that can crush ice.

Glassware

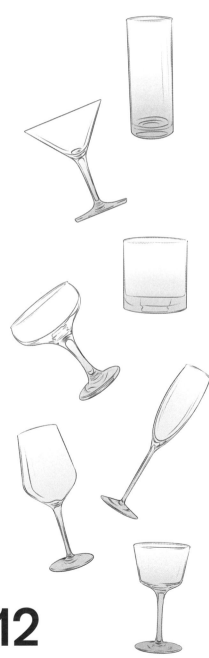

Half the fun of cocktails is in the presentation, and glassware is a big part of that. Many cocktails are traditionally served in a certain type of glass; a good example is the Martini glass, made to suit its namesake drink. You don't have to be dogmatic about glassware, though; there's always room for experimentation, and sometimes you'll see cocktails being served in vessels that weren't originally meant for cocktails at all.

Highball / Collins glass
Highball and Collins glasses are very similar and are often used interchangeably. Both are tall, narrow glasses meant for serving mixed drinks (though the Collins glass is somewhat narrower and taller).

Martini / cocktail glass
Like highball and Collins glasses, Martini and cocktail glasses look similar, though the cocktail glass is a bit smaller. They're conical in shape and meant for cocktails served straight up without ice.

Rocks glass
Rocks glasses (also called Old Fashioned or lowball glasses) are short and typically used for drinks served on ice—hence the name.

Coupe
Coupe glasses were originally designed to serve champagne, but the wide mouth isn't that great for bubbles. Today, they're a popular choice for mixed drinks served straight up.

Champagne flute
Flutes are tall, slender glasses with small mouths designed to retain the bubbles in sparkling drinks. They're great for any cocktail made with sparkling wine.

Wine glass
Sometimes, you might want to serve a cocktail in a wine glass, particularly if it contains wine. You can use one with a stem, or go stemless.

Nick and Nora glass
Somewhere between a coupe and a cocktail glass, the Nick and Nora glass is a small, elegant stemmed glass with a slightly narrower rim than either of its competitors. Use it for any drink served straight up.

Copita glass
The copita, a tulip-shaped glass originally meant for sherry (and these days often used for whiskey), can be used for cocktails too.

Copa de balon glass
A stemmed, globe-shaped glass that resembles a red wine glass, the copa de balon is typically used for bubbly drinks like Spanish-style gin and tonics, Portuguese Porto Tónicos, or Aperol Spritzes.

Mint Julep cup
Mint Juleps are traditionally served in a metal tumbler that gets nice and frosty due to the icy cold drink within.

Tiki mugs and glasses
Retro-tropical tiki bars have their own particular types of glassware. The most common are tiki mugs or glasses molded in the shape of Polynesian tiki carvings or other tropical shapes such as pineapples. Tiki drinks, in turn, tend to feature tropical flavors like pineapple, coconut, and rum, and are often quite strong.

Mugs
Hot drinks are sometimes served in mugs (often clear) with a handle, or insulated glassware.

Beer glass
You might serve a beer-based drink in a beer glass, though you can always get more creative.

Mason jar
Mason jars are used for canning and preserving food but, lately, they've become a hip vessel for serving cocktails. Bonus: if you pop a lid on, you can take your drink with you for a picnic.

Cocktail Ingredients

Cocktails rely on the skillful layering of flavors to create a beautiful, balanced, and delicious drink. These are some of the ingredients you'll use.

Alcoholic spirits

Most cocktails contain alcohol, which comes in many different varieties. You can learn about them in detail in the Types of Alcohol section.

Infused alcohols

Infused alcohols can heighten the complexity of your cocktail. All you need is a neutral liquor (vodka is the most common alcohol used in infusions, but you can infuse basically anything) and a complementary flavor. Combine your flavoring and your alcohol in a clean, airtight container (such as a Mason jar), seal tightly, and leave somewhere cool and dark until the liquor has absorbed enough flavor. Strain out the flavoring, and store in an airtight container again. Some ingredients, like jalapeño peppers, don't need much time to infuse at all—just a few hours—while others (ginger, lemongrass) need up to a week.

Non-alcoholic spirits

People who don't consume alcohol can still enjoy interesting non-alcoholic cocktails, and booze-free spirits can help. The OG non-alcoholic distilled spirit is Seedlip, which comes in different flavor profiles to complement various zero-proof concoctions. Other producers mimic specific types of alcohol: you can try Monday gin, Lyre's dark cane spirit in place of rum, or Ritual zero-proof tequila, to name just a few. Still, non-alcoholic spirits may be best considered their own category rather than a 1:1 replacement: cocktails are all about balance, and it's a good idea to experiment to make sure everything in your drink is working in harmony.

Citrus juices

Many cocktail recipes involve citrus juice (usually lemon or lime). *Always* use fresh juice—it tastes better, and all you need is a cheap hand-held squeezer.

Simple syrup

Simple syrup is a sugar-and-water mixture used to sweeten cocktails. The most common version uses a 1:1 ratio of sugar to water, though some recipes call for a "rich" simple syrup that uses a 2:1 ratio. To make it, add sugar and water to a saucepan, heat on medium heat until the sugar is dissolved and the liquid is clear, then take off the heat and allow to cool. You can store it in the fridge for up to a month. See pages 142–43 for detailed recipes for different flavored syrups.

Shrubs

Shrubs are sweet, fruit-based drinking vinegars that bring an acidic tartness to cocktails. You can make shrubs via a "hot" or a "cold" method. The hot method is similar to making a flavored simple syrup—you simmer fresh fruit in sugar water and then add vinegar—while for the cold method, you toss fresh fruit in sugar, allow it to sit, and add vinegar to the syrup that forms. The cold method has a brighter, fruitier flavor, while the hot method tastes a bit more like jam.

Eggs and foamers

Some cocktail recipes call for egg whites to create a silky foam at the top of the drink. It's best to use fresh eggs for this, and you can separate the white from the yolk using a slotted spoon. But if you're vegan or don't like consuming raw eggs, you can substitute in aquafaba, a fancy-sounding word that refers to the liquid—which is typically discarded—found in a can of chickpeas. Just sub in the same measure of aquafaba as you would use of egg whites (a typical egg white is about 1 oz / 30 ml).

Dairy

Some cocktails (especially dessert cocktails, but also frothy drinks like the Ramos Gin Fizz) include dairy—typically cream, which is richer and less prone to curdling than milk. If you're vegan, rich nut milks and coconut cream can make good substitutes.

Bitters

Cocktail bitters are flavorings added to mixed drinks in drops or dashes to create more complex flavor profiles. There are different types of bitters: aromatic (strong botanical flavors; Angostura bitters are an aromatic), citrus (orange is the most common), herbal, spice, fruit, and nut.

Types of Alcohol

A cocktail's personality is partially dictated by the kind of alcohol it contains. Even within a type, there's a lot of variation—premium brands may taste different from more budget-friendly varieties, and if you explore small distilleries close to home (encouraged!) you'll find even more local character.

One key thing to remember for a delicious cocktail is to use alcohol that hasn't expired; a decade-old dusty bottle from the back of your parents' liquor cabinet will probably not make the best tipple. As a rule of thumb, you should consume hard alcohol within a year; it won't become unsafe to drink after that, but it will begin to lose both flavor and alcohol content. Any fortified wines or alcohols under 15% ABV should be stored in the fridge after opening—and while you can keep them for a while that way, even refrigerated fortified wines should be consumed within three months. Just think of it as an incentive to experiment widely with the same bottle—or share with friends.

Here are a few of the most common types of alcohol you'll encounter in this book.

Whiskey
Nobody can agree on how to spell whiskey (or, whisky), but its rich flavor makes it one of the most popular kinds of liquor used in cocktails. Whiskey is distilled from different types of grain—barley, corn, rye, and wheat—and then aged in oak barrels. The most common are Scotch (malted grain whiskies made in Scotland and aged for a minimum of three years), bourbon (American whiskeys made from corn), and rye (made from rye, and often produced in Canada or the USA). Famous whiskey cocktails include the Old Fashioned, the Manhattan, and the Whiskey Sour.

Gin
Gin is a clear alcohol defined by the flavor of juniper berries. Some gins add juniper post-distillation, while others (distilled gins and London dry gins) involve it in the distillation process. While gin has to taste predominantly of juniper in order to be considered gin, it often features other botanical flavors too, including citrus, anise, coriander, cucumber, and rose petals. It's a favorite with bartenders, and you can find it in drinks like the Negroni, Martini, and French 75.

Rum and cachaça

Rum is distilled from sugarcane or molasses and has a rich, sugary flavor. There are many different varieties, from light rum (which is basically clear) to dark rum (which is full-bodied, and often consumed straight up). It's predominantly produced in the Caribbean and Latin America, and is often used in cocktails with a tropical flavor: Mai Tais, Mojitos, and Daiquiris. A close cousin to rum is cachaça, which is produced in Brazil from fermented sugarcane juice and used in Caipirinhas.

Vodka

Vodka is the most neutral spirit, clear and almost flavorless. It's made from fermented potatoes and grains, and while it's often associated with Russia, most of it is produced elsewhere: Sweden, Finland, Poland, France, and the United States are among the leading vodka hotspots. Famous vodka cocktails include the Moscow Mule, Bloody Mary, and Vodka Martini.

Tequila and mezcal

Mexico's national spirit is distilled from the blue agave plant, and its production is centered around the town that inspired its name, Tequila. There are different types, ranging from blanco (which is clear and unaged) to añejo (aged for a minimum of one year, with a rich amber color). Tequila is technically a type of mezcal, a similar beverage also made with agave (though not blue agave). Unlike tequila, mezcal has a distinctive, smoky flavor. You can find tequila and mezcal in cocktails like the Margarita and Paloma.

Brandy

Brandy is a distilled wine made from different types of fruit, sometimes aged in casks. The most famous brandy is Cognac, which is produced in pot stills in a specific region of France, around the town of Cognac. Other examples include pisco, a clear, grape-based brandy famously associated with Peru and Chile; calvados, a French apple brandy; kirsch, a clear, dry German brandy made from cherries; and grappa, an Italian apple brandy. In this book, when the word "brandy" is used generically, it typically refers to Cognac-style grape brandies, while recipes that use pisco, calvados, grappa, or kirsch will refer to them specifically. Cocktails incorporating brandy include the Brandy Alexander and Sidecar (Cognac) and Pisco Sour (pisco).

Fortified wines

Fortified wines are wines which have had their alcohol content boosted by adding a distilled spirit, such as brandy. Some examples of fortified wines include port, made in Portugal, and which can be found in ruby, tawny, and white varieties, and sherry, a Spanish fortified wine whose varieties include the light and dry fino, the still dry but more complex and aged amontillado, and the dark and rich oloroso. Some fortified wines, known as aromatized wines, have been flavored with herbs and spices for more complexity. Examples of those include vermouth, which is flavored with botanicals and comes in both dry and sweet varieties, and Lillet, a French aperitif fortified with citrus liqueur which comes in several varieties, the most popular of which is Lillet Blanc. You can find fortified wines in many cocktails: vermouth is especially versatile and features in the Martini, Manhattan, and Negroni, and sherry is essential in a Sherry Cobbler. Port can be found in the Porto Tónico or as a float on a New York Sour, while Lillet appears in a Vesper and white Negronis.

Amari

Distinct from cocktail bitters, which are concentrated bitters added by the dash, digestif and aperitif bitters, or amari (the plural of amaro, which is Italian for "bitter"), are spirits flavored with bitter roots and herbs, traditionally used to stimulate the appetite or digestion (before and after a meal, respectively) or used as a hangover cure. They also bring complexity to many cocktails. The most easygoing and popular are the intense red Campari and sweet, orangey-red Aperol, but other examples include the sweet, dark Averna and the bright yellow gentian bitter Suze. Cocktails that rely on bitters include the Negroni (which uses Campari) and the Aperol Spritz.

Liqueurs

Liqueurs are sweet, flavored alcoholic beverages, and there's an almost endless variety of them to suit your every cocktail whim. Examples include the widely used triple sec, which has a bright, orange flavor; crème de cassis, a sweet, jammy liqueur made from blackcurrants; amaretto, a liqueur made from almonds or apricot kernels that tastes a lot like marzipan; and maraschino, a liqueur made from distilling Marasca cherries along with their pits, which gives it a bitter nuttiness. While liqueurs appear in countless cocktails, you can specifically find triple sec in a Margarita or a Mai Tai; crème de cassis in a Kir Royale; amaretto in an Amaretto Sour; and maraschino in an Aviation.

Cocktails for Dietary Restrictions

Here are some considerations for crafting delicious drinks for the most common dietary restrictions.

Vegan
Most alcohol is vegan, but there are exceptions. Alcohol made from honey—mead, as well as some gins and vodkas—is not. Cream-based liqueurs like Bailey's are also not vegan. Kahlua, which contains sugar filtered with bone char, often takes people by surprise. (You can sub the vegan friendly coffee liqueur Mr. Black.) You can check the vegan status of any liquor on the comprehensive vegan web reference Barnivore.

Most non-vegan cocktail ingredients have easy substitutes: instead of egg white as a foamer, you can use 1 oz (30 ml) aquafaba, the reserved liquid from canned chickpeas. For creamy cocktails, you can substitute coconut cream or a rich nut milk. And if you want to make a vegan Bloody Mary, you'll need to sub out the Worcestershire sauce since it includes anchovies—but you can find store-bought vegan varieties or make your own.

Alcohol-free
The world of zero-proof cocktails has flourished in recent years. You can experiment with non-alcoholic spirits; some of them attempt to mimic the flavors of distilled alcohols like whiskey, gin, rum, and tequila (Lyre's and Ritual are examples), while others have their own unique flavor profiles (like Seedlip).

But you don't need to purchase zero-proof spirits to make a good cocktail. There are other ways to bring sophistication to your drinks. Shrubs offer a pleasing tang, while syrups with floral, bitter, smoky or woody flavors (lavender or rosewater, cardamom, vanilla, cinnamon, or any variety of tea) can bring complexity. Muddled herbs, meanwhile, can lend your concoctions a fresh herbaceousness.

Gluten-free
Nearly all distilled alcohol is gluten-free, even when made from barley, wheat, and rye. The one distilled alcohol you might need to watch out for is ouzo, which can involve additional grains post-distillation.

Beer, which is not distilled, is not gluten-free—so if you plan to make beer cocktails, you'll need to source a gluten-free beer. As always, it's best to double-check the label—especially for flavors added post-brewing.

Garnishes and Rims

Garnishes and rims are the accessories of the cocktail world; they help dress up a tipple and finish its look. They're an easy way to make even the most basic drink look special.

Citrus
The most common and versatile garnishes are citrus fruits. You can try adding a citrus wheel—a thin, circular cross-section of the entire fruit cut with a knife—for a fun, tropical feel, or a citrus wedge (that familiar bar garnish) if you want to squeeze the juice into your drink. A citrus twist is the classiest of the bunch; to make one, slice off a thin strip of citrus peel using a knife or a peeler, twist it or wrap it around a straw to give it a spiral shape, then drape over the rim of a glass. It's quick, sophisticated, and adds both the aroma and flavor of citrus oil to your drink.

Fruit
Citrus isn't the only fruit garnish in town. You can use almost any kind of fruit as a garnish, including cherries, pineapple, apples, and strawberries. Cut a vertical slice in the fruit and mount it on the side of the glass, or skewer it on a cocktail pick and lay it across the top.

Edible flowers
Flowers bring a lush, botanical aesthetic to your drink. There are many different types of edible flowers, including common garden flowers like cornflowers, nasturtiums, pansies, squash blossoms, and dandelions. If you don't feel like foraging through your flowerbed, specialty grocery stores often sell edible flowers in the fresh herbs section.

Herbs
Herb garnishes can range from understated (an elegant sprig of rosemary) to downright wild and overgrown (several bunches of mint or basil). Herbs don't just look pretty: they also add an intoxicating aroma to your cocktail, which you'll inhale each time you take a sip. Before you add an herb garnish, press on the leaves to release their essential oils—but not so hard that you crush them.

Straws
Ditch the plastic (the oceans don't need it) and opt for reusable stainless steel or glass straws. They look much classier, too.

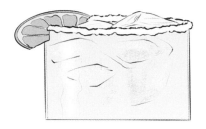

Rims
Your first experience with a cocktail rim was likely the salted edge of a Margarita glass, but there are other options, too. You can use either sugar or salt, and experiment with mixing in other herbs and spices (try a chili salt mixture, or cinnamon sugar). To rim a glass, pour the salt or sugar onto a plate in a thin layer, run a lime or lemon around the edge of your glass, and then dip the glass into the rimming mixture.

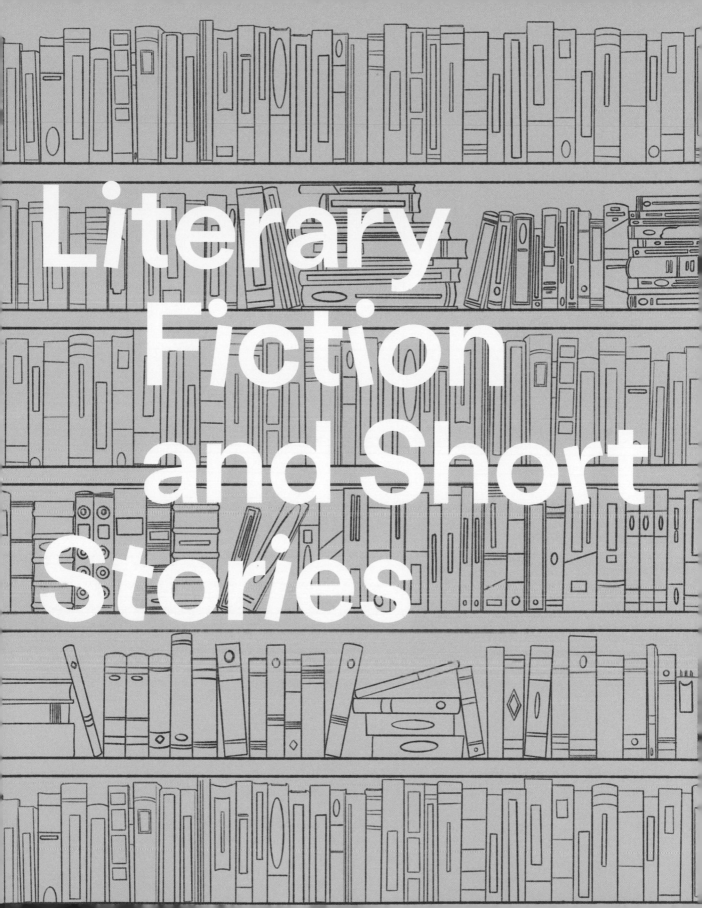

Literary Fiction and Short Stories

Literary fiction written by women—both novels and short stories—is a vast and varied body of work impossible to fully capture in a single short description. One thing some (though not all) women writers of fiction do is center female protagonists in their stories. Many write characters who represent a community they understand, broadening the scope of the types of people we see in fiction. Others undertake meticulous research to accurately depict characters and stories outside their own orbit.

The writers in this section represent just a small selection of the influential world of fiction by women. Ranging from Jane Austen, who wrote witty novels about women's dependence on marriage in the 19th century, to Toni Morrison, who blazed a trail for Black writers beginning in the 1970s; from Amy Tan, who, since the '80s, has brought the experiences of immigrant mothers and first-generation daughters to the page, to Torrey Peters, a contemporary writer who pens funny, touching novels featuring transgender characters, the writers in these pages run the gamut in terms of lives lived and their style on the page. Their creativity offers fertile inspiration for tribute cocktails, all of which tap into the rich imagination required to dream up fictional landscapes.

Toni Morrison

The Toni Morrison

2   shots gin
¾   shot blueberry syrup
     (p. 142)
½   shot heavy cream
½   shot fresh lemon juice
½   shot fresh lime juice
1   egg white
1–2 shots club soda
     (soda water) to top
Garnish: dehydrated
     citrus wheel

Add all ingredients
except club soda to
a shaker without ice and
shake vigorously for 30
seconds. Add ice and shake
for another 30 seconds.
Strain into a Collins glass
(without ice), top with
club soda until foam peeks
over the top, and garnish.

One of the giants of contemporary literature, Toni Morrison inspired a generation of Black writers, first in her work as an influential editor, and then as a prizewinning author.

Morrison—born Chloe Ardelia Wofford—grew up in a working-class home in Ohio. Her love for storytelling began at family gatherings listening to folk tales and ghost stories. She was a voracious reader, absorbing works by Jane Austen, Leo Tolstoy, and others. At age 12, she converted to Catholicism, taking the baptismal name of Anthony—which friends shortened to "Toni." Morrison's parents worked extra jobs to send their academically gifted daughter to college. Aspiring to be "surrounded by Black intellectuals," she studied at Howard and then Cornell.

Morrison went on to teach college English and married an architect named Harold Morrison, but after the marriage fell apart, she assumed a job as a textbook editor to support her two children. On the side, she wrote a novel titled *The Bluest Eye*. The story of a Black woman who yearns for blue eyes, the novel caught the attention of Morrison's employer, Random House, who made her a fiction editor. In her 19 years of editing, she nurtured an impressive list of Black writers, including Toni Cade Bambara, Angela Davis, and Muhammad Ali.

While she edited, Morrison continued to publish her own books, such as *Song of Solomon*, which won the National Book Critics Circle Award and brought her enough recognition to pursue writing full-time. In 1987, she published her masterwork, *Beloved*, a viscerally written historical novel about a formerly enslaved Black woman haunted by her dead daughter. It won the Pulitzer and also the Nobel Prize for Literature (with Morrison its first Black woman recipient), and has become an American classic.

Morrison's towering presence is embodied by this imposing, complex, delightful gin fizz.

Virginia Woolf

The Virginia Woolf

2   shots oaked amber rum
¾   shot peach syrup
     (p. 143)
¾   shot fresh lemon juice
Garnish: mint

Add all ingredients to a shaker filled with ice and shake vigorously. Strain through a fine strainer into a Nick and Nora glass. Gently press mint with fingers to release oils, and garnish.

Literary modernism is, to many, synonymous with Virginia Woolf. The innovative prose stylist introduced the world to stream-of-consciousness fiction—and, simultaneously, argued for a space for women in the literary sphere.

Woolf's freedom to pursue literature came from financial independence, something unusual for women of her era and a topic she explored in her writing. She grew up in a privileged, well-educated family and attended King's College in London, where she befriended a number of high-profile feminists. By the time she was 23, she was writing for the *Times Literary Supplement* and associating with the Bloomsbury Group, a circle of avant-garde artists and intellectuals who rebelled against Victorian society and rejected bourgeois ideals (including those of heteronormativity). In 1909, when she was 27, her aunt passed away and left her a significant inheritance—a windfall that gave her the freedom to write, unfettered. Twenty years later, as a celebrated author, she published an essay titled "A Room of One's Own," which explores how the confined social and financial roles of women dampened their ability to create, and, in particular, to write fiction.

Woolf's other famous works—mostly fiction—remain just as relevant. *Mrs. Dalloway* explores a single day in the life of a woman, probing the boundaries of one's inner world and the postwar social structure. *To the Lighthouse* centers on a family's summer home on the Isle of Skye in Scotland: it is a philosophical novel that uses omniscient narration to examine the complexity of experience and human relationships. And *Orlando*, inspired by Woolf's romance with the novelist Vita Sackville-West, features a protagonist who lives for centuries and switches from male to female midway through life. It's a book that feels particularly modern today, in an era when ideas of gender are being probed and upended.

The main character in *Orlando* spends nearly 300 years writing a poem titled "The Oak Tree," exploring both identity and literary history. The cocktail dedicated to Woolf finds its roots with an oaked rum and a clean, modern finish.

Zadie Smith

The Zadie Smith

¾ shot St-Germain
½ shot Suze
4   shots champagne
<u>Garnish</u>: baby's breath

Pour St-Germain and Suze
into a large wine glass
filled with ice. Top with
champagne and garnish.

British novelist, essayist, and short story writer Zadie Smith is acclaimed for her broad, sweeping novels that deftly examine race, class, cultural identity, and celebrity.

Smith grew up in Northwest London in public housing projects, the child of a Black Jamaican mother and a white English father. She attended a state school, and later studied English at the University of Cambridge, making money as a cabaret singer on the side. Before she graduated, short stories she'd included in a student anthology attracted the notice of publishers, motivating Smith to find an agent. Her debut novel, *White Teeth*, which told the story of three culturally diverse families whose lives intersect in London, sold at auction based on the first 100 pages. When it was published to widespread critical and popular acclaim in 2000, she was held up as an icon of modern-day Britain, able to interpret the culture and also represent it.

Over the following decades, Smith continued to publish masterful, considered books, both fiction and essays, to a rapt fanbase. Her awards include winning the Women's Prize for Fiction twice, for both her wildly successful *On Beauty* (which was also shortlisted for the Booker) and *NW*. Her novel *Swing Time*, which drew upon her love of jazz and tap dancing and told the story of a Kylie Minogue-inspired pop star and her personal assistant, was also shortlisted for the Booker.

Smith's fame transcends literary stardom—her glamour (on top of her intellect) has landed her in the pages of *Vogue* and on the red carpet at the Met Gala, and she's recognized as a style icon and role model for creative women. Still, she's best judged by her work; as she told the *Guardian* in 2011, "There is no 'writer's lifestyle.' All that matters is what you leave on the page."

The cocktail dedicated to Smith is elegant and sophisticated, much like the author and her writing.

Sally Rooney

The Sally Rooney

2   shots Irish whiskey
¾   shot fresh lemon juice
¾   shot basic simple syrup
      (p. 142)
2   dashes Angostura
      bitters
1   shot whole milk
      (at least 3.5%),
      for clarifying
Garnish: dehydrated
orange wheel

Stir whiskey, lemon juice, basic simple syrup, and bitters in a mixing glass. Pour mixture into milk in a second mixing glass. Leave for one hour to curdle.

Strain curdled mixture through a coffee filter. Pour over a clear ice cube in a rocks glass and garnish.

A keen observer of human relationships, Irish novelist Sally Rooney is a virtuoso at bringing modern intimacy to the page.

Rooney is known for writing characters whose lives are similar to her own. She grew up in the town of Castlebar, the daughter of a telecom worker and an arts center administrator. Her anti-authoritarian streak meant she didn't enjoy school, but she applied herself in other ways: by age 15, she'd written her first book ("absolute trash," she says today). Later, she was accepted to study English Literature at Trinity College in Dublin, where she also became a member of the debate team. During her master's degree, Rooney spent three months completing a draft of the novel *Conversations with Friends*. It was only after the publication of an essay she wrote about her debating experience, "Even If You Beat Me," that she came to the attention of a literary agent. *Conversations with Friends* sold in a seven-way auction and was published to great fanfare in 2017 when she was only 26.

Normal People, Rooney's second novel, pushed her fame into the stratosphere. Published in 2018, it chronicles a tortured, on-and-off romance between school friends, tapping into Millennial angst about noncommittal relationships and titillating the reading public with the book's numerous steamy-but-realistic sex scenes. And, in 2021, Rooney published her third novel, *Beautiful World, Where Are You*—about relationships, but also about a writer struggling with fame, class, and a world on the brink of collapse.

Rooney writes in a clear, clean style that deserves a cocktail to match. The drink dedicated to her is a clarified Whiskey Sour featuring Irish whiskey—a beverage whose elegance relies on familiar ingredients being presented in a particularly compelling manner.

Amy Tan

The Amy Tan

1½	shots white rum
6	raspberries
¾	shot Campari
¾	shot fresh lime juice
½	shot basic simple syrup (p. 142)

Garnish: lime peel

Add white rum and
raspberries to a shaker.
Muddle thoroughly.
Add other ingredients,
add ice, shake, and
strain into a coupe glass.
Garnish with lime peel
carved into the shape of
a leaf.

Intergenerational relationships in Chinese American families are at the heart of Amy Tan's body of work. The bestselling novelist was one of the first to bring stories of Asian American lives to a broad, mainstream audience.

Tan was born in Oakland, California, and raised by Chinese immigrant parents. Her childhood wasn't easy: when she was fifteen her father and her brother died of brain tumors, and she had a strained relationship with her mother, who often threatened to kill herself. After running away with a boyfriend of whom her mother didn't approve (and whom Tan would later marry), she completed degrees in English and Linguistics and became a successful freelance business writer. However, success took its toll, and to escape the grind of 90-hour weeks, she began writing fiction and joined a writers' workshop. She published her first short story a year later, which captured the attention of an agent, and went on to pull together a proposal for a book.

Around the same time, Tan traveled to China with her mother, resolving to learn more about her. Upon her return, her agent had landed her a deal for her first book: *The Joy Luck Club*, which was partially inspired by Tan's own life. A novel of interlinking vignettes about Chinese immigrant mothers and their American daughters (and stories told over games of mahjong), it spent over forty weeks on the *New York Times* bestsellers list, was a finalist for the National Book Award, and was eventually adapted into a film. Tan followed it with several other bestselling novels, usually featuring complex relationships between mothers and daughters, including *The Kitchen God's Wife*, *The Hundred Secret Senses*, *The Bonesetter's Daughter*, and *The Valley of Amazement*. In 2017, she published a memoir, *Where the Past Begins: A Writer's Memoir*, at the urging of her editor.

The cocktail dedicated to Tan is a vibrant red, an auspicious color within Chinese culture that carries symbolic meaning in *The Joy Luck Club*.

Harper Lee

The Harper Lee

6   blackberries
2   shots tequila
1   shot vanilla syrup
     (p. 143)
1   shot fresh lime juice
1   shot club soda
     (soda water)
<u>Garnish</u>: daylily

In a shaker without ice, muddle blackberries with all the other ingredients except club soda. Add ice, shake, and fine strain into a rocks glass over ice. Top with club soda and garnish.

Rarely has a single book made such a profound mark on culture as Harper Lee's *To Kill a Mockingbird*. Its portrayal of racial injustice through the eyes of a girl in the Southern US inspired empathy in readers and made Lee a household name.

Born in Alabama, Lee was a precocious reader with a big imagination, and spent summers with her friend, the future author Truman Capote. They wrote stories together on a typewriter, and the strong, tomboyish Lee would beat up Capote's bullies. When Lee was 10, she witnessed an event that haunted her: her lawyer father defended two Black men accused of murdering a white shopkeeper; the men were found guilty and hanged.

Later, Lee dropped out of law school to join Capote in New York, where they pursued their dreams of becoming writers. Lee assembled a manuscript (titled *Go Set a Watchman*), which, after extensive rewrites, was published as *To Kill a Mockingbird*. Inspired by her childhood, the book is told from the perspective of a young white girl, Scout, whose father, a lawyer named Atticus Finch, defends a Black man falsely accused of rape. An appealing story with a strong moral message, the book was an instant, massive hit, selling millions of copies and winning the Pulitzer Prize.

Lee didn't enjoy fame and stopped giving interviews four years after the book's publication. A year before her death, a second novel was published under her name: *Go Set a Watchman*, a sort-of sequel to *Mockingbird* based on its first draft. Its release was controversial, partially because some doubted that Lee truly wanted to publish the book.

Multiple cocktails have been inspired by *To Kill a Mockingbird*, most with the pun-y name "Tequila Mockingbird." The first, originating in the 1960s, includes tequila, lime, and crème de menthe. This cocktail also involves tequila, as well as Alabama's state fruit (the blackberry!)—but it's dedicated to the unconventional, brilliant Lee herself.

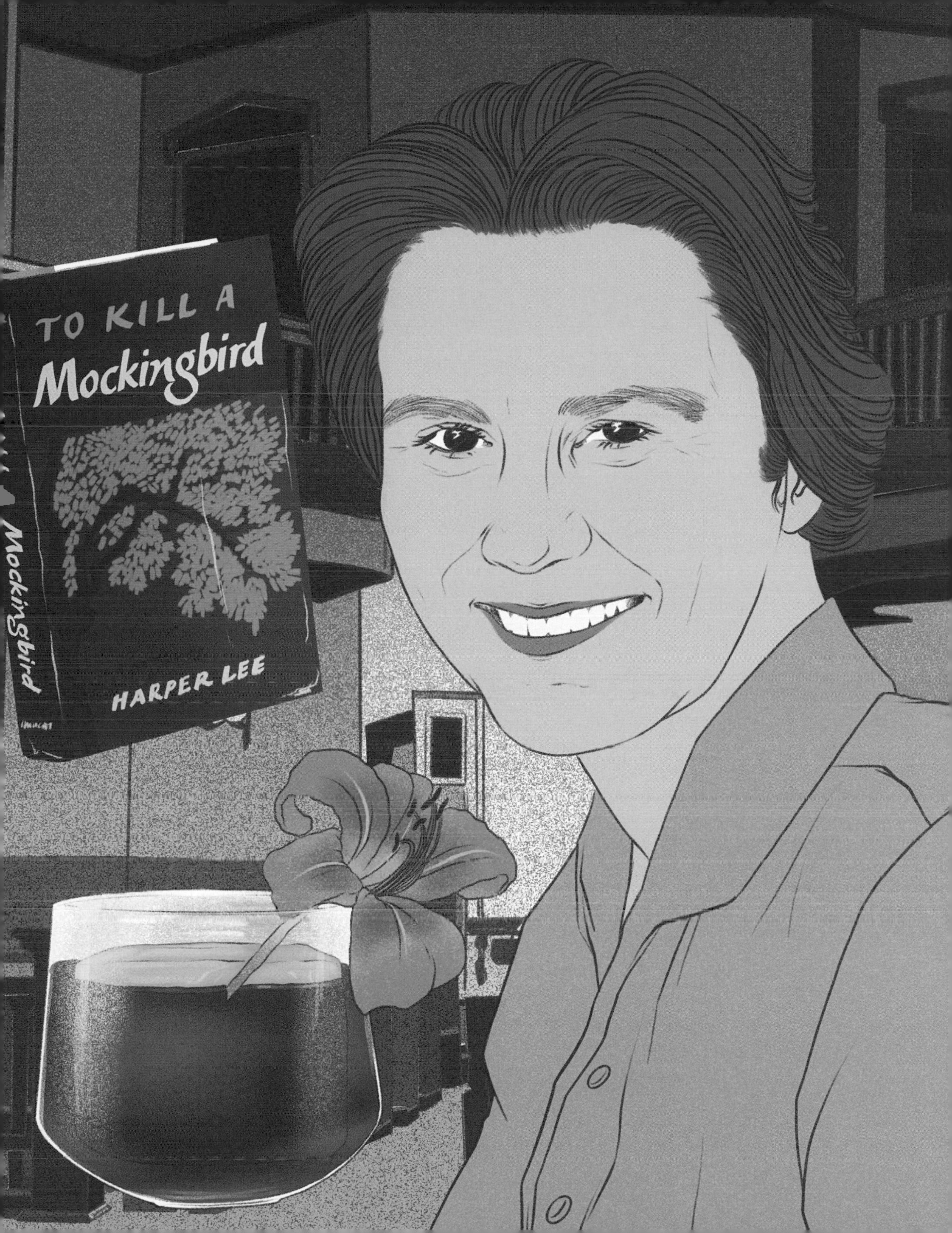
TO KILL A
Mockingbird
HARPER LEE
Mockingbird

Bernardine Evaristo

The Bernardine Evaristo

2   shots strawberry-and-
    lime-infused gin
    (p. 144)
1   shot dry vermouth
Garnish: lime twist

Add ingredients to a mixing
glass with ice. Stir,
strain into a chilled
Martini glass, and garnish.

Bernardine Evaristo is renowned for her portrayal of the diverse lives of Black British women, as well as her unconventional, poetic prose.

Evaristo grew up in a large family in Southeast London with a white English mother and Nigerian immigrant father. As a mixed-race child in 1960s Britain, she experienced discrimination and taunts, which caused her to develop a toughness she now sees as essential to her creative perseverance. The tomboyish Evaristo's early creative outlet was theater, which she started practicing at age 12. After failing to get into the National Youth Theatre, she studied theater at Rose Bruford College and collaborated in setting up a company, the Theatre of Black Women, which was dedicated to exploring their underrepresented experiences.

Evaristo's path to literary success was a long and winding one. In her early thirties, after exiting an abusive relationship with an older woman who co-opted and suppressed her efforts to perform and publish poetry, she released her first volume, *Island of Abraham*. She published her first novel, *Lara*, based on her family's story, in 1997; written in poetic verse, it was what Evaristo came to call "fusion fiction." Her second novel, 2001's *The Emperor's Babe*, used a similar style and told the story of Zuleika, a Black girl who comes of age in Roman London. 2008's *Blonde Roots*, shortlisted for the Orange Prize, ranged into satire, exploring an alternative world where Africans enslaved Europeans. Yet, despite some recognition, writing was not lucrative for Evaristo, and she had to maintain side jobs in arts administration to pay the bills. That changed dramatically when she published *Girl, Woman, Other*, a fusion fiction novel loosely linking the stories of 12 Black British women. It won the 2019 Booker Prize (in a controversial joint prize, won alongside Margaret Atwood), making Evaristo the first Black woman and first Black Briton to receive the award. Now, she is a household name, and continues to use her position to advocate for recognition for Black women.

Evaristo's drink is a fusion cocktail: it's a Martini in the style of a Strawberry Daiquiri.

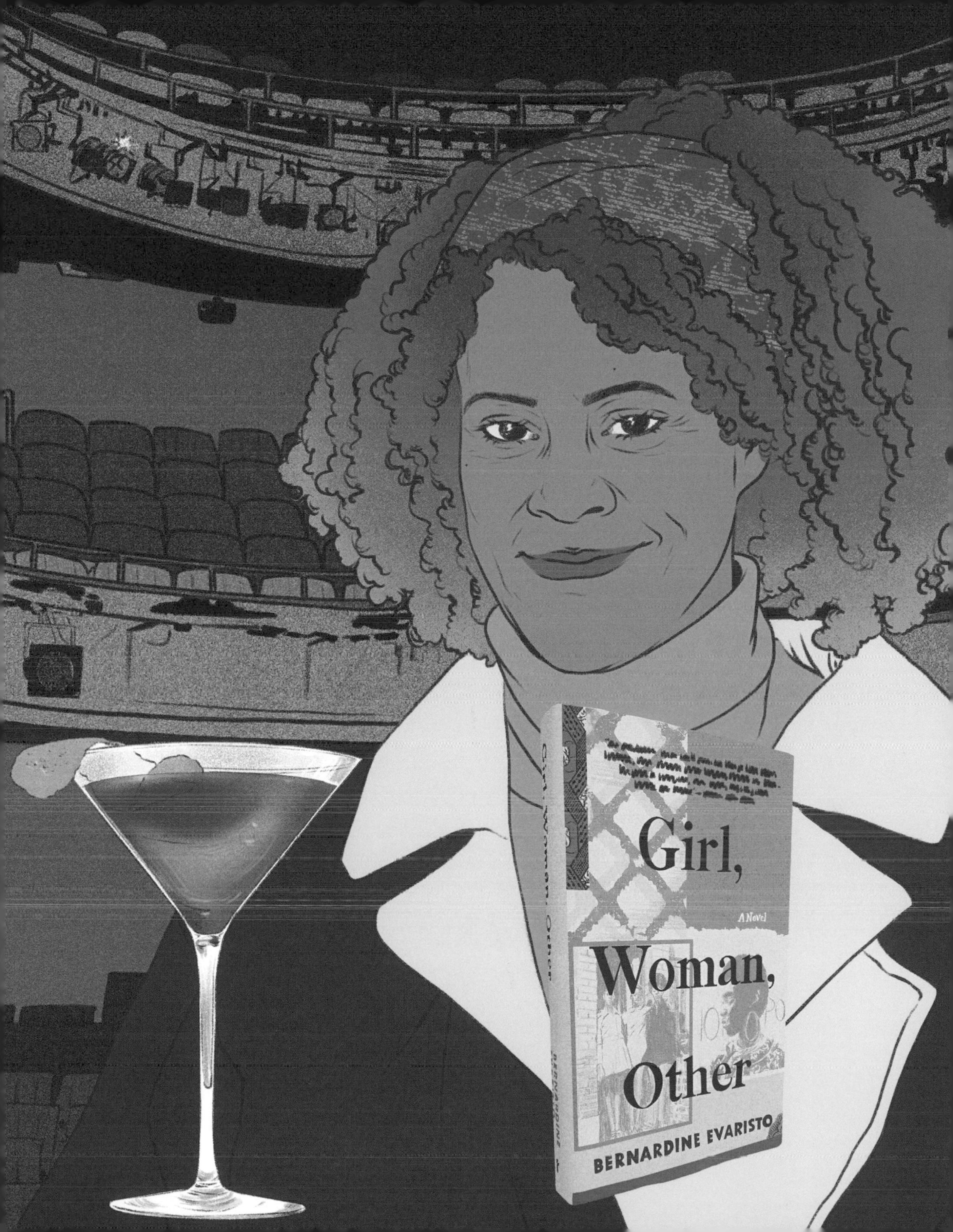
Girl,
A Novel
Woman,
Other
BERNARDINE EVARISTO

Jhumpa Lahiri

The Jhumpa Lahiri*

¾ shot raspberry shrub
    (p. 144)
¾ shot fresh lemon juice
3   shots prosecco
3   shots club soda
    (soda water)

<u>Garnish</u>: lemon wheels and
a sprig of rosemary

Add raspberry shrub and
lemon juice to a shaker
with ice. Shake and strain
into a copa de balon glass
filled with ice. Add
prosecco and club soda,
stir gently, and garnish.

*   This is a low-proof
cocktail.

Jhumpa Lahiri's writing explores what it means to be caught between cultures—and between languages.

Lahiri was born in London and grew up in Rhode Island in the US, and when she was small, her Indian-born parents often took her to Kolkata to immerse her in her family heritage. When she was in kindergarten, her teacher had difficulties pronouncing her given name, Nilanjana, and called her by her nickname, Jhumpa—which sparked feelings of conflict in the future author about identity. Still, she thrived in school, and attained several degrees, including two MAs, an MFA, and a PhD from Boston University.

Like many writers, Lahiri faced multiple rejections early in her career, though she did place short stories in magazines and literary reviews. When she published her debut short story collection, *Interpreter of Maladies*, in 1999, any uncertainties about success vanished: the book won the Pulitzer Prize and went on to sell millions of copies. Themed around the immigrant experience and feelings of dislocation, it resonated with a wide range of readers for its poignant depictions of human connection. She followed that with a novel, *The Namesake*, which told the tale of a child who, much like Lahiri herself, has complicated feelings about his nickname.

Lahiri always felt conflict between English and the Bengali spoken by her parents, and in 2015, she made a fresh start by beginning to write in Italian, a language she mastered after moving to Rome. Her first books in Italian, including her memoir about learning the language, *In Other Words*, were translated into English by Ann Goldstein (who's best known as Elena Ferrante's translator). But Lahiri also became a translator in her own right, notably adapting Italian author Domenico Starnone into English. In 2021, she translated *Whereabouts*, the first novel she wrote and published in Italian, into English, cementing her bond with her chosen language.

The cocktail dedicated to Lahiri is a zesty Italian spritz that's decidedly on its own path.

b. 1963

Donna Tartt

The Donna Tartt*

3   lemon wheels
     (1 for garnish)
½   shot blueberry syrup
     (p. 142)
2   shots 10-year
     tawny port
<u>Garnish</u>: mint and
blueberries

Muddle 2 lemon wheels
and blueberry syrup in
a shaker. Add ice and port
and shake vigorously.
Strain into a rocks glass
filled with crushed ice,
and garnish with the
remaining lemon wheel,
mint, and blueberries.

*   This is a low-proof
cocktail.

A mysterious intellectual who spends a decade writing each of her novels, Donna Tartt defies celebrity and devotes herself fully to her craft.

Tartt grew up on the Mississippi Delta with a rockabilly-musician-turned-politician father and an uninterested Southern belle mother. A precocious reader and grammarian, she began writing stories at age five and published her first poem at 13. As a teen, she worked at the local library and devoured books, especially those by Charles Dickens. She was discovered by the writer Willie Morris in her first year of studies at the University of Mississippi, and two years later, at his urging, she transferred to the elite liberal arts college Bennington. There, she studied classics, and became close friends with another future literary star, Bret Easton Ellis, to whom she would dedicate her first novel, *The Secret History*.

After a heated bidding war that ended with Knopf buying the book for $450,000, it was published in 1992 to public spectacle. Tartt received an eight-page interview in *Vanity Fair* magazine that proclaimed her fame—but she quickly realized she didn't enjoy the spotlight. Still, her suspense novel about a circle of classics students at a New England liberal arts college who commit a murder found a huge audience, and Tartt was able to retreat into the background once again. She has largely remained there, granting few interviews, simply emerging every 10 years to publish a new magnum opus. Her second book, *The Little Friend*, published in 2002, tells the story of a girl in the South who endeavors to solve her brother's murder. And, in 2013, she released *The Goldfinch*, a sweeping, 771-page novel about a child who survives a terrorist bombing at an art museum and, in the fray, steals a painting called *The Goldfinch*. The book polarized reviewers, but was a bestseller that won the 2014 Pulitzer Prize.

Tartt's cocktail involves a port aged ten years, the length of time she takes to craft her novels.

Celeste Ng

The Celeste Ng

1	shot white rum
1	shot golden rum
1	shot fresh lime juice
¾	shot lychee liqueur
½	shot orgeat syrup

<u>Garnish</u>: flaming lime

Add all ingredients to a shaker filled with ice. Shake vigorously and strain into a rocks glass filled with crushed ice. Garnish with a flaming lime by placing a 151-proof-rum-soaked sugar cube inside half a spent lime, and lighting the sugar cube on fire.

Complex family relationships and racial dynamics in America set the stage for drama in Celeste Ng's novels. Exploring themes of class, race, and privilege, her writing reveals truths about the world while delivering an emotional payoff.

Ng was born in Pittsburgh and, when she was 10, her family moved to the wealthy suburb of Shaker Heights outside Cleveland, Ohio. As a teen, she was co-editor of her high school's literary magazine, and later studied English at Harvard. It wasn't until after she graduated that she seriously considered writing as a career, which prompted her to get an MFA from the University of Michigan. Success didn't come until Ng won the Pushcart Prize for her story "Girls, at Play." Soon after that, she sold her first book, *Everything I Never Told You*, a breakthrough debut chosen as Amazon's novel of the year. It unravels the story of a mixed-race family whose daughter drowns, revealing the forces that led to her death.

Ng's second novel, *Little Fires Everywhere*, was a huge bestseller that was adapted into a television series of the same name, starring Reese Witherspoon and Kerry Washington. Set in Ng's hometown of Shaker Heights, the book explores motherhood, transracial adoption, racism, and classism within a privileged community. (The fires in the title refer to multiple blazes an unidentified arsonist sets in the family home of the main protagonists.) Ng's third novel, *Our Missing Hearts*, is her foray into dystopia, creating a world much like our own where laws intended to "preserve American culture" permit the seizing of dissidents' children and censorship of "unpatriotic" books.

Outside of writing, Ng is a fierce advocate for other authors and generously blurbs books, especially those of Asian American women, whose voices are underrepresented in publishing. As she told the *New York Times* in 2018, "There are lots of other Asian women, even Chinese-American women, who are doing all kinds of stuff that I'm not doing."

Ng's cocktail packs a powerful punch and comes garnished with a little fire.

Louise Erdrich

The Louise Erdrich**

2   wild strawberries,
     sliced
1   shot juniper-cardamom
     syrup (p. 142)
1   shot fresh lemon juice
4   shots club soda
     (soda water)
Garnish: rosemary and
a lemon wheel

Place strawberries in
the bottom of a Collins
glass, and pour in juniper-
cardamom syrup and lemon
juice. Using a muddler,
muddle strawberries
thoroughly. Add ice cubes
to top of glass and top
with club soda. Garnish and
serve with a glass straw.

** This is a zero-proof
cocktail.

Pulitzer Prize-winning writer Louise Erdrich is one
of the most prominent figures of the Native American
Renaissance. Best known for novels richly populated
with Indigenous characters, her work often weaves
issues of social justice into suspenseful, multilayered
narratives.

Erdrich was born in Minnesota in 1954, the daughter
of a German American father and a Chippewa mother,
and grew up in North Dakota. Her grandfather was the
chairman of the Turtle Mountain Band, and as a child,
she would visit relatives on the reservation. A writer
since she was young, Erdrich pursued an English degree
at Dartmouth College at the same time as it launched
a Native American studies department, where she began
to research her family history. She later pursued
an MA in writing at Johns Hopkins, using elements of
her ancestry as inspiration for her creative process.

After winning prizes for her poems and short
stories, Erdrich published her first novel, *Love
Medicine*, which follows five Ojibwe families living
on reservations in North Dakota and Minnesota. The
book won the National Book Critics Circle Award in
1984, heralding her arrival as a literary force. Most
of her following novels are set in similar Indigenous
communities in the same geographic area, creating
a rich fictional representation of place that has led
some to compare her to William Faulkner. In 2021,
Erdrich was recognized with the Pulitzer Prize for
Fiction for her novel *The Night Watchman*, inspired
by her grandfather's fight against the US government's
campaign of "termination," which would have ended
federal recognition of Indigenous nations and forced
them to assimilate.

Her relationship with the literary world extends
beyond writing. She also owns a bookstore, Birchbark
Books, in Minneapolis, catering to the "Indigirati"
(Indigenous literati) with a focus on Indigenous writing
and art.

Erdrich's cocktail incorporates the woodsy taste
of juniper berries and flavorful wild strawberries.

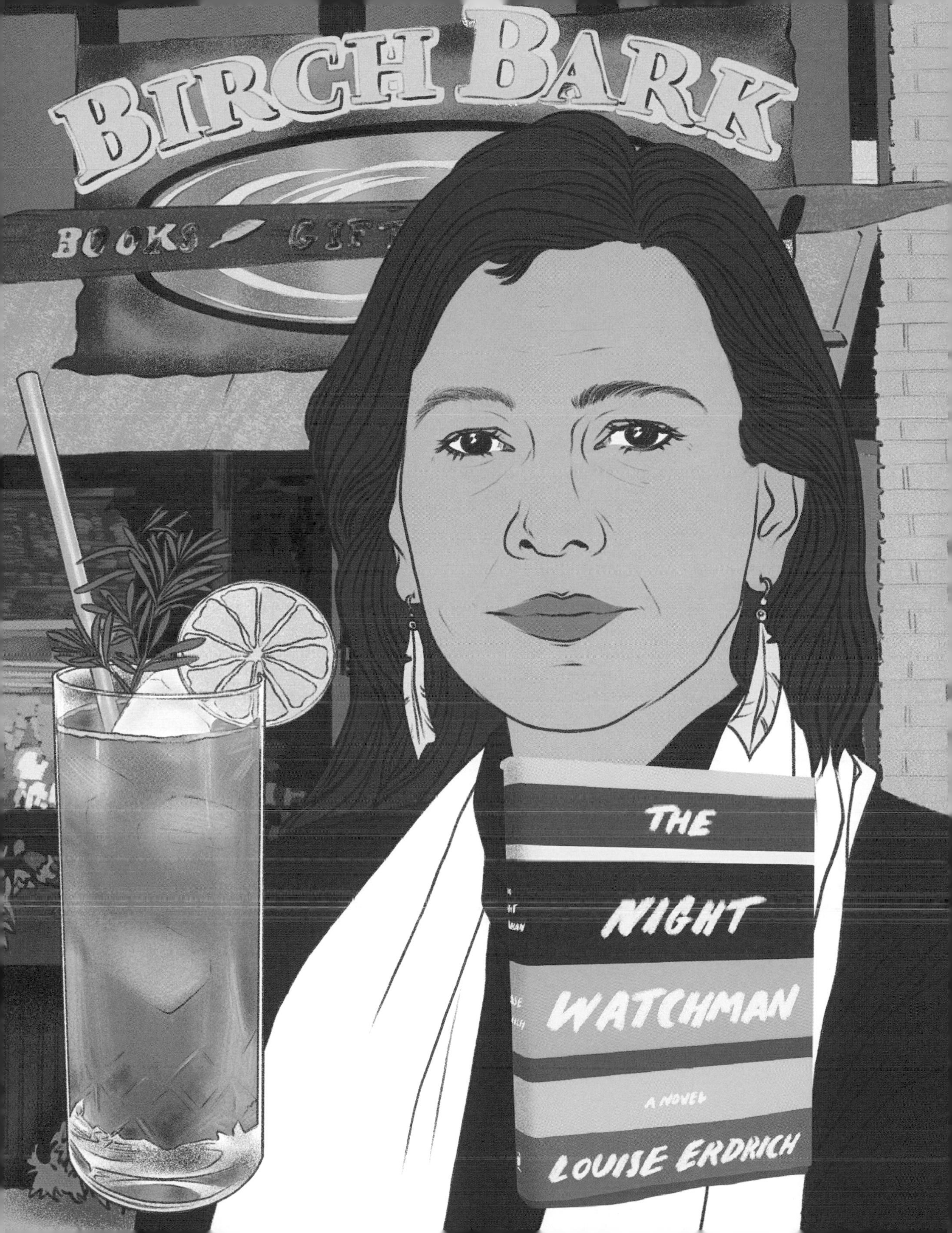
BIRCH BARK
BOOKS
THE NIGHT WATCHMAN
A NOVEL
LOUISE ERDRICH

Torrey Peters

The Torrey Peters

1½ shots hibiscus-
     infused white rum
     (p. 143)
1   shot coconut water
½   shot orgeat syrup
½   shot fresh lime juice
½   shot pineapple juice
1   shot aquafaba
Garnish: pineapple leaves
and orchid

Add all ingredients to
a shaker filled with ice.
Shake vigorously, strain
into a coupe glass,
and garnish.

Torrey Peters' fiction revolves around the lives of transgender women. Her stories don't follow expected narratives of social justice—because she centers trans women as her subjects and her audience, she produces writing that's vivid, risky, and real.

Peters grew up in Chicago, attended a Quaker boarding school as a child, and, as an adult, obtained an MFA from the University of Iowa. Later, while completing an MA in Comparative Literature at Dartmouth, she transitioned. Soon after, she became involved in the edgy, DIY trans writing scene that revolved around the indie publisher Topside Press, and self-published two novellas—*The Masker* and *Infect Your Friends and Loved Ones*—which she offered as free downloads to other trans women. Her work caught the attention of major publishers, who wanted to know if she had a novel. She did: *Detransition, Baby* was published in early 2021, to major mainstream success.

The novel focuses on a trans woman, Reese; her detransitioned ex, Ames; and the cis partner (and boss!) he's made pregnant, Katrina—and the idea that they might all raise a child together. Tackling big questions about motherhood, gender, and family, the book was longlisted for both the PEN/Hemingway Award and the Women's Prize for Fiction, and Peters was praised for her willingness to write about topics some might consider taboo.

When she's not engaged in literary pursuits, Peters rides her motorcycle around Brooklyn—a Kawasaki, which she painted pink to dissuade men from assuming it might be a boyfriend's bike. Her cocktail is hot pink, too.

Jane Austen

The Jane Austen

1½ shots gin
1   shot honey syrup
    (p. 143)
¾ shot fresh lemon juice
1   1-inch (2.5 cm) piece
    of ginger, sliced
2   shots club soda
    (soda water)
<u>Garnish</u>: lemon twist

Add gin, honey syrup, lemon juice, and ginger to a shaker. Muddle ginger. Add ice, shake, and strain into a coupe glass. Top with club soda and garnish.

Jane Austen's nuanced understanding of human behavior enabled her to write novels that remain cherished classics more than 200 years after their publication. Her naturalistic treatment of domestic life—unusual at the time—placed women at the center of literature, while her deft use of irony and subtle social commentary won her critical acclaim.

Austen's young life was quiet; she was mostly educated at home, reading widely from her clergyman father's library. She broadened her horizons by visiting her older brothers, one of whom inherited a large sum of money and introduced her to the world of the landed gentry (which would inform her novels). She began writing comic stories when she was 11, and penned her first novella at age 19.

Austen's novels are all set against the backdrop of Georgian society, featuring women negotiating class and the pursuit of marriage. Austen didn't manage to find a publisher until 1811, for *Sense and Sensibility*. *Pride and Prejudice*, *Mansfield Park*, and *Emma* were published in succession soon after, and two more books were released posthumously. While her novels were moderately successful during her lifetime, she wasn't famous. Women's accepted roles were those of wife and mother, and most female authors published anonymously—including Austen.

It wasn't until the 1880s that she became popular under her own name, with so-called "Austenolatry" gripping passionate fans, while more cliquish and intellectual "Janeites" railed against the hoi polloi's claim on their hero. Austen's fandom has only grown into the present day, amplified by popular adaptations of her work, such as the classic 1995 BBC TV version of *Pride and Prejudice* (featuring Colin Firth as Mr. Darcy) and the film *Clueless*, based on *Emma* (starring Alicia Silverstone). As one of the most beloved writers of all time, Austen is also featured on the English £10 note—the only woman aside from the late Queen Elizabeth currently honored.

Austen was also a home brewer who made both beer and mead; her cocktail borrows the flavor profile of mead in tribute to what she liked to drink.

b. 1968

Min Jin Lee

The Min Jin Lee*

2   shots soju
1   shot yuzu juice
     (fresh yuzu is hard
     to find outside Asia,
     so this recipe uses
     pre-packaged)
½   shot basic simple syrup
     (p. 142)
Garnish: lemon twist

Add all ingredients to
a shaker with ice. Shake
vigorously, strain into
a cocktail glass, and
garnish with a lemon twist.

*   This is a low-proof
cocktail due to soju's low
alcohol percentage.

Min Jin Lee's meticulously researched, sprawling novels sensitively portray the lives of people across the Korean diaspora.

Lee was born in Seoul, South Korea, and her family emigrated to Queens, New York, when she was seven years old. Moving to America was a shock: in Seoul her family had been solidly middle class, but in New York, her father ran a newspaper stand and then a jewelry store, and the family had to work their way up the social ladder. After attending the specialized Bronx High School of Science, she pursued a history degree from Yale and also studied law at Georgetown. She spent two years working as a corporate lawyer, but it was draining work, and Lee—who then had a liver disease that could have ended her life early—decided to quit to pursue her dream of writing.

She opens each of her novels with a "thesis statement"; for her debut, 2007's *Free Food for Millionaires*, it was "Competence can be a curse," in reference to high-functioning people and the laser focus that can blind them. The book tells the story of a second-generation Korean woman striving in New York high finance; as part of Lee's research, she interviewed scores of people from Harvard Business School and took a class there herself. The thesis statement for 2017's *Pachinko* was "History has failed us, but no matter"— pointing to the way poor people have been ignored and devalued, but how they persevere. *Pachinko* (named after the Japanese gambling machine) is an epic story tracing three generations of a Korean family living under Japanese rule and oppression—and was the first novel published in English about Korean Japanese people. As part of her research process, Lee interviewed many Korean-Japanese people in Japan to get their story right. The novel was nominated for a National Book Award, and in 2022, it was adapted into a popular Apple TV series.

Lee's cocktail combines a mix of Korean flavors into something new.

Sheila Heti

The Sheila Heti

6	large basil leaves (one for garnish)
2	shots pisco
¾	shot fresh lime juice
½	shot basic simple syrup (p. 142)

Add 5 basil leaves, pisco, lime juice, and basic simple syrup to a shaker. Muddle basil vigorously with a muddler until pulverized. Add ice, shake, and fine strain into a Nick and Nora glass. Garnish with remaining basil leaf.

The philosophical, experimental novelist Sheila Heti writes books that ask (but maybe don't directly answer) difficult questions. Because her protagonists sometimes lead lives resembling her own, she's also been heralded as one of the foremost authors of autofiction.

Heti grew up in an upper-middle-class neighborhood in Toronto, the child of two Hungarian Jewish immigrants. As a teen, she rebelled against her strait-laced environs by fashioning herself as a libertine, and cites the provocative novelists Henry Miller and the Marquis de Sade as influences. After high school, she studied playwriting in Montreal and art history and philosophy back in Toronto.

Heti published her first book, a collection of short stories, when she was 24. But it was her fifth book (and second novel), *How Should a Person Be?*, that electrified the literary world with its strange, meandering, and humorous exploration of the "best" way to live. Heti, supposedly inspired by the reality television show *The Hills*, portrayed her artistic characters—one named Sheila, and others named after her real-life friends—documenting the amusing and profound banalities of life and asking questions about how to make great art. The novel landed her on numerous best-of lists, including a *New York Times* list of "The New Vanguard," their 2012 list of notable books, and a longlisting for the Women's Prize for Fiction. Heti's next major book, *Motherhood*, was equally attention-grabbing. Another foray into autofiction, it interrogates, from the perspective of a protagonist very similar to Heti, the question of whether to have a child and how that choice affects women's ability to create. It was shortlisted for the Giller Prize and named book of the year by *New York* magazine.

The cocktail dedicated to Heti is inspired by the green leaf that plays a pivotal role in her surreal, fable-like 2022 novel, *Pure Colour*.

Isabel Allende

The Isabel Allende

2	shots pisco
½	shot crème de violette
¼	shot orgeat syrup
¾	shot fresh lime juice

Garnish: micro star flowers

Add all ingredients to a shaker filled with ice. Shake vigorously, fine strain into a Nick and Nora glass, and garnish.

Isabel Allende's magical realist fiction is populated by strong, complicated women (who sometimes possess paranormal powers) making interesting choices as they navigate their lives.

Allende was born into an upper-middle-class home in Lima, Peru, but after her father left the family, they relocated to live with her grandparents in Santiago, Chile. There, growing up, she witnessed her grandmother leading seances and trying to move objects with her mind—cementing Allende's belief that reality is up for interpretation. As an adult, she became a journalist, working at a feminist magazine and writing a column critiquing machismo culture called "Civilize Your Troglodyte." She also briefly worked as a translator of romance novels—a job she was fired from after she made unapproved creative changes to plots to make female protagonists appear more independent and intelligent.

In 1970, Allende's uncle, a socialist politician named Salvador Allende, was elected president of Chile. Three years later, he took his own life when Chile was taken over by the brutal military junta of Augusto Pinochet. Allende herself narrowly escaped assassination and fled to Venezuela, where she lived in exile for 13 years. The shakeup freed her from traditional notions of what her role in society should be, and fueled her need to write. In exile, she penned her first novel (which many consider her best), *The House of the Spirits*. Intended as a letter to her dying grandfather and meant to exorcize the ghosts of the Pinochet dictatorship, the book was initially rejected by multiple publishers. Eventually, Allende found a publisher in Buenos Aires, and the book became a massive success. Since then, she has started writing every one of her novels on the same date she began her first, January 8—a habit she began as a superstition, and which became a form of personal discipline.

With a career spanning multiple decades and more than twenty books, Allende is now recognized as the world's most widely read Spanish-language author. She won Chile's National Prize for Literature in 2010, and in 2014, President Barack Obama awarded Allende, who now resides in California, the Presidential Medal of Freedom.

Her cocktail is complicated, floral, and maybe just a little bit magic.

b. 1959

Arundhati Roy

The Arundhati Roy

2 shots spice-infused gin
   (p. 144)
1½ shots basic simple
   syrup (p. 142)
½ shot fresh lemon juice
½ shot fresh lime juice
3 shots club soda
   (soda water)
Sliced strawberries,
mangoes, cucumber,
lemons, limes
Garnish: 1 bunch mint

Add ice to a Collins glass.
Pour in spice-infused
gin, basic simple syrup,
and lemon and lime juice.
Add sliced strawberries,
mangoes, cucumber, lemons,
and limes. Top with club
soda, garnish, and serve
with a steel straw.

Social justice is at the heart of Arundhati Roy's writing. Best-known for her novel *The God of Small Things*, she has spent most of her career as an activist.

Roy grew up in the tropical southwestern Indian state of Kerala in the care of her mother, a divorced women's rights activist. She left home at 16 and moved to Delhi, where she squatted in slums; living there cemented her empathy for vulnerable populations. In college she studied architecture and began writing screenplays. She started writing a novel in 1992 loosely inspired by her life in Kerala, which she published in 1997. Titled *The God of Small Things*, it told, in lyrical prose, the story of fraternal twins whose lives are torn apart by "Love Laws" dictated by social class. The book's success was staggering: it won the Booker Prize and became the best-selling book published in English by a non-expatriate Indian author, turning Roy into a celebrity.

She defied expectations that she would quickly publish another novel, turning her attention for two decades to political writing and activism. Roy put her support behind the Kashmiri separatist movement, opposed American military intervention in Afghanistan, and advocated for environmental causes—in the process becoming known as an intellectual and polemicist. A selection of her many essays was published as the 2019 collection *My Seditious Heart*. In a 2014 *New York Times Magazine* article, she expressed frustration at people saying she hadn't written in 20 years: "As if all the nonfiction I've written is not writing," she said. But she made her much-anticipated return to fiction in 2017, with *The Ministry of Utmost Happiness*, another novel that embodied her politics, telling the story of characters navigating dark moments in India's history.

The cocktail dedicated to Roy is infused with Indian spices and garnished with refreshing summer fruits.

b. 1977

Chimamanda Ngozi Adichie

The Chimamanda Ngozi Adichie*

1 shot Campari
½ shot grenadine
½ shot fresh lime juice
½ shot fresh lemon juice
½ shot fresh orange juice
1 bar spoon Angostura bitters
4 shots club soda (soda water)
Garnish: thin slices of cucumber, lime, and lemon

Add all ingredients except club soda to a shaker filled with ice. Shake vigorously and strain into a Collins glass filled with ice. Garnish, top with club soda, and serve with a glass straw.

* This is a low-proof cocktail.

Chimamanda Ngozi Adichie is one of the most prominent African writers of contemporary fiction. Her work, both serious and humorous, deals with issues of race, gender, and the complexities of identity between America and Africa.

Adichie was born into a large Igbo family in Nigeria and grew up in the college town of Nsukka, where both her father and her mother worked at the University of Nigeria (as a professor and registrar, respectively). Her family's home was the former house of the famous Nigerian writer Chinua Achebe. As a child, reading Achebe's books demonstrated to Adichie that there was a place for Africans in literature.

When she was young, it was expected that good students would pursue careers in the professions. Thus, Adichie spent her first two years at the University of Nigeria studying medicine before she won a scholarship to study communications in the United States; she moved there at age 19. Feeling homesick during her senior year, she wrote her first novel, *Purple Hibiscus*, about postcolonial Nigeria. Two years later, she published *Half of a Yellow Sun*, set during the Nigerian Civil War in Biafra, which won the Orange Prize (now the Women's Prize for Fiction).

Adichie is best known for her 2013 novel, *Americanah*, which centers on a Nigerian woman who finds fame in the United States writing about race—specifically, how Americans view Blackness. She won the National Book Critics Circle Award, and the book appeared on many best-of lists. In the same year, part of a TED talk she gave, "We should all be feminists," was sampled by Beyoncé for her song "Flawless," bringing Adichie another level of popularity and fame.

The cocktail dedicated to her is inspired by a drink called the Chapman, known as "Nigerian sangria."

Joyce Carol Oates

The Joyce Carol Oates

2   shots mezcal
1   shot tamarind purée
¾   shot basic simple
     syrup (p. 142)
½   shot fresh lime juice
<u>Rim</u>: Tajín

Add all ingredients to a shaker full of ice. Shake vigorously and strain into a rocks glass with ice, rimmed with Tajín.

Joyce Carol Oates explores darkness, violence, and social unrest in her vast and varied body of work. One of the most accomplished American authors of our era, she challenges convention with her writing.

Oates grew up on her parents' farm in upstate New York, a rural area hard hit by the Great Depression. She studied in a one-room schoolhouse and found joy in reading, burying herself in the work of writers like Fyodor Dostoyevsky and the Brontë sisters. When she was 14, her grandmother gave her a typewriter, and she began to write. In 1962, after she completed a master's degree, she taught at the University of Detroit, witnessing the social upheaval of the era. She published her first short story collection and a novel soon after.

One of Oates' most enduringly famous works, the short story "Where Are You Going, Where Have You Been?", was published in 1966. Based on the serial killer Charles Schmid, it tells the story of a teenage girl pulled into the orbit of a predatory man. Oates began her Wonderland Quartet soon after; all the novels were finalists for the National Book Award, but *them* won it. Set in Detroit, it deals with violence, drugs, and racial conflict in the working class. Perhaps her most famous novel, *We Were the Mulvaneys*, was released in 1996; chosen for Oprah's Book Club, it portrays how a rape tears apart an American family. Oates' nonfiction work is also notable—including *On Boxing*, a collection of essays about a complicated, violent sport that she is passionate and knowledgeable about.

Oates is famous for her productivity: she writes (in longhand) beginning in the early morning, sometimes skipping breakfast. She has published dozens of novels and hundreds of short stories, a number that has flummoxed critics. In the present day, she channels some of her energy online, where she is an enthusiastic (and sometimes controversial) presence on Twitter; she even has her own Substack.

The cocktail dedicated to Oates is strong, spicy, and a little challenging, just like her work.

Zora Neale Hurston

The Zora Neale Hurston

6	basil leaves
2	strawberries, sliced
¼	shot basic simple syrup (p. 142)
2	shots bourbon

Garnish: basil sprig

In a Mint Julep cup, thoroughly muddle basil and strawberries with basic simple syrup. Pack glass with crushed ice and add bourbon. Stir, and top with more ice. Garnish and serve with a steel straw.

An unparalleled expert in the Black vernacular and ethnography, Zora Neale Hurston is one of the most recognized names of the Harlem Renaissance.

Hurston was born in Alabama but grew up in Eatonville, Florida, an all-Black township where her sense of self was bolstered by a culture where all positions of power and influence were held by Black people. She led a happy childhood until her mother died and, after feuding with her father's new wife, left home to work with a traveling Gilbert and Sullivan theater troupe. At age 26, she decided to finish high school, and subtracted 10 years from her age to do it for free.

Flourishing in academia, in college Hurston pursued research in ethnography and traveled to the American South, Jamaica, and Haiti to research local cultural practices. She followed that with graduate studies at Columbia University. While living in Harlem, she associated with Harlem Renaissance writers such as Langston Hughes, and turned her apartment into a favorite party location (though she sometimes wrote in her bedroom while guests reveled).

Hurston's major successes came from her mid-forties on. Her best-known novel, *Their Eyes Were Watching God*, was published in 1937; written in a well-crafted vernacular, it tells the story of a Southern Black woman's search for self through three marriages. An example of her nonfiction, *Tell My Horse*, published in 1938, explored voodoo in the Caribbean. Still, she never received financial success to match her acclaim, and when she passed away she was buried in an unmarked grave in Florida. In 1973, Pulitzer Prize-winning novelist Alice Walker (now best known for *The Color Purple*) published an essay in *Ms. Magazine* in which she searched for Hurston's grave. The renewed interest in Hurston elevated *Their Eyes Were Watching God* into the literary canon.

The drink dedicated to Hurston is a spin on a Mint Julep—a Southern drink that, though many may not know it, was popularized by a Black bartender.

S. E. Hinton

The S. E. Hinton

3 shots prosecco
1 shot turmeric-infused
 vodka (p. 144)
½ cup (110 ml)
 pineapple sorbet
Garnish: mint

Add all ingredients to
a mixing glass and stir
until combined. Pour
into a champagne flute
and garnish.

As a teenager, S. E. Hinton wrote to portray the realities of the world around her. Her first book, *The Outsiders*, paved the way for an entirely new genre: young adult fiction.

Susan Eloise Hinton was born in Tulsa, Oklahoma, and as a child, dreamed of becoming a rancher; when she began to write stories, they were about cowboys and gunfighting. As a book-loving teen she was dissatisfied with the fiction—largely teen romance—available to people her age. Inspired by events at her high school, where there was a bitter war between rival gangs, the working-class Greasers and the upper-class Socials (or "Socs"), she wrote a book, *The Outsiders*. Hinton showed the book to a friend's mother, a children's author, who introduced her to an agent. When the book sold to Vintage, Hinton's publisher counseled her to publish under her initials, S. E., to avoid sexist dismissal by reviewers who thought a girl wouldn't know about teen violence.

Published in 1963, *The Outsiders* explicitly targeted teens as its audience, who were drawn in by its memorable characters and themes of class-based injustice. Despite controversy (some tried to ban it), it was adopted in classrooms and became a bestseller. Fame gave Hinton a difficult case of writer's block, but after gentle encouragement from her boyfriend (who told her to write two pages at a time), she completed a second book, *That Was Then, This Is Now*. She followed that with three more YA novels: *Rumble Fish*, *Tex*, and *Taming the Star Runner*. In the 1980s, a high-school teacher sent a petition signed by her seventh- and eighth-grade students to the director Francis Ford Coppola, asking him to adapt *The Outsiders*. He did, and the film versions of that book and *Rumble Fish* further cemented their status as American classics.

One of the most memorable lines from *The Outsiders*, "Stay gold, Ponyboy, stay gold," urges the story's main character, Ponyboy, to hold onto his youthful innocence. The cocktail dedicated to Hinton is gold, too.

Sayaka Murata

The Sayaka Murata*

1   shot fresh lemon juice
1   shot ginger syrup
    (p. 142)
6   shots Sapporo lager
5   shots club soda
    (soda water)
Garnish: lemon wheel

Add lemon juice and ginger syrup to a shaker. Shake and fine strain into a beer glass. Top with Sapporo and club soda, stir gently, and garnish.

*   This is a low-proof cocktail.

Social norms within Japanese society—and the nonconformists who break them—are the focus of Sayaka Murata's cult-venerated body of writing.

Murata was born in Chiba Prefecture, just outside of Tokyo, in a conservative, middle-class home. She was raised to conform to traditional gender roles: her brother was encouraged to become a doctor or judge, while she was groomed to be a wife. She tried hard to blend in and avoid offending anyone, and didn't have an outlet for her real thoughts until she found writing; she penned her first novel when she was in fourth grade. After high school, she studied the arts at university, and took a part-time gig at a convenience store—a job she worked for 18 years.

Murata's first published novel, 2003's *Jyunyū* (*Breastfeeding*), won the Gunzo Prize for New Writers. From that point on, she published prodigiously, favoring themes of gender roles and discrimination, motherhood, and sex (or, more often, celibacy and asexuality). Murata's tenth novel, *Konbini ningen*, won the Akutagawa Prize (one of Japan's most prestigious literary awards) in 2016; it was translated into English and published as *Convenience Store Woman* in 2018, becoming a bestseller. Telling the story of a 36-year-old virgin who rejects society's expectations to marry and have children and instead finds satisfaction in the predictable environs of a convenience store, Murata struck a nerve with her depiction of the narrowness of women's roles in society. Murata herself continued to work in the convenience store where she found her inspiration—until the attentions of an obsessed fan forced her to leave her job.

Since the success of *Convenience Store Woman*, Murata's works have continued to be published in English. *Earthlings*, published in 2020, is a dystopian novel about a girl who believes she's an alien and views society as a factory—which then ends on a note of horror. And in 2022, she published a new collection of short stories, *Life Ceremony: Stories*.

Murata's cocktail is inspired by convenience store beer and soda.

Elena Ferrante

The Elena Ferrante

1½   shots Averna
¾   shot bourbon
1   shot fresh lemon juice
¼   shot basic simple syrup
     (p. 142)
1   egg white
<u>Garnish</u>: cherry

Add all ingredients to
a shaker without ice and
dry shake for 10 seconds.
Add ice and shake for
another 10 seconds. Strain
into a coupe glass and
garnish with a cherry on
a cocktail pick.

Pseudonymous Italian author Elena Ferrante tests the question of how important a writer's identity is to the work they create. Though her novels about the lives of Italian girls and women are a global sensation, she has steadfastly maintained her anonymity, preferring that her writing take center stage.

Ferrante's first novel, *Troubling Love*, was published in Italian in 1992, and right from the start, she chose to preserve her privacy rather than cultivate a public life. That became more challenging once her Neapolitan Quartet of novels was translated and published in English, beginning with *My Brilliant Friend* in 2012, followed by *The Story of a New Name*, *Those Who Leave and Those Who Stay*, and *The Story of the Lost Child*. The books follow best friends Elena ("Lenù") Greco and Raffaella ("Lila") Cerullo from childhood to old age as they navigate the social hierarchies, violence, and politics of Naples. Sweeping and detailed novels that were praised for their perceptive portrayals of the complicated rivalries in female friendships, the Neapolitan Quartet built Ferrante a passionate following of millions of fans who would obsess over release dates and character arcs—and eventually over who, exactly, the enigmatic author might really be. Theories circulated; some thought she was actually a man (a claim that Ferrante dismissed as a sexist underestimation of women's writing as weak). In 2016, an investigative journalist tracked her royalty payments and concluded that she was a literary translator and editor who works for Ferrante's Italian publisher. Many were appalled by the investigation, calling it a violation of privacy. Still, in the years since, questions of who she might be have faded into the background, with readers happy to experience her novels for what they are: complex, layered, unapologetic chronicles of the female experience.

Ferrante's cocktail is also layered and complex, and includes the quintessential Italian amaro, Averna.

Poetry

Poetry is one of the oldest forms of literature. Women's voices in the genre reach back as far as ancient Greece, when Sappho wrote her famous verses of lesbian love and desire. Some of the most innovative and avant-garde poets have been women—one only needs to look to Emily Dickinson for evidence of that. Women poets have found the words to galvanize a nation, as evidenced by inaugural poets Maya Angelou and Amanda Gorman. Others have harnessed the power of poetry to connect with the masses—Rupi Kaur and Mary Oliver, while focusing on totally different subjects, have found the sort of rock-star success that isn't typically associated with poets.

The poets in this book are unbound by subject matter and form. While many have tried to characterize what, exactly, "women's poetry" might be, these writers are proof that it's impossible to define—but a joy to read. Representing a genre where every word is a specific creative choice, these poets inspire cocktails where every ingredient is carefully considered for effect.

Maya Angelou

The Maya Angelou

1½ shots oloroso sherry
¾ shot Kahlua
1 egg
Garnish: coffee bean

Add ingredients to a shaker
with no ice. Shake hard to
emulsify. Add ice and shake
vigorously for at least
30 seconds. Strain into
a copita glass and garnish.

Memoirist and poet Maya Angelou centered her own life
in her body of work, making space for the experiences
of Black Americans to be taken seriously in literature.
Born Marguerite Johnson in St. Louis, Missouri,
Angelou's early life was tumultuous. She and her brother
were shuttled between the care of different relatives,
and she was abused by her mother's boyfriend. When
he was murdered, likely by her uncles, Angelou believed
it was her speaking up that had killed him. She was
silent for five years, using her voice again only after
a teacher who encouraged her love for reading told
her, "You do not love poetry, not until you speak it."
Angelou had a child at 17 and married, but when
her marriage ended, she became a professional dancer,
changing her name to the more mellifluous Maya Angelou.
She toured in the cast of *Porgy and Bess* and even
released an album of calypso songs. In 1959, she moved
to New York to focus more on her writing, becoming
part of the Harlem Writers Guild. She also began
to flourish as an activist, working as a coordinator
for the Southern Christian Leadership Conference with
Martin Luther King, Jr. By 1969, she published her
first memoir, *I Know Why the Caged Bird Sings*, which
chronicled how she used literature to triumph over
racism and trauma. The book's success propelled Angelou
to literary stardom, paving the way for a further
six memoirs. She was also a prolific poet, and her work,
which earned her the sobriquet of "the Black woman's
poet laureate," was nominated for a Pulitzer Prize.
In 1993, she was the first Black American and the first
woman to perform at a presidential inauguration, for
President Bill Clinton. The recording of the poem won
her a Grammy.
Angelou liked to write with a glass of sherry in
hand. Her drink is a flip, a drink that, in the
19th century, was said to "give strength to delicate
people"—much like Angelou's writing.

Maya Angelou
I Know Why the Caged Bird Sings
I Know Why the Caged Bird Sings
Maya Angelou

Emily Dickinson

The Emily Dickinson*

1½ shots bianco vermouth
     (note: NOT dry white
     vermouth)
1   shot fresh lemon juice
1   shot egg white
½   shot flower syrup
     (p. 142)
Garnish: daisies

Add all ingredients to
a shaker filled with ice.
Shake vigorously and strain
into a Nick and Nora glass.
Garnish.

*   This is a low-proof
cocktail.

Emily Dickinson's rejection of convention made her one of the most notable poets of the modern era. A recluse who saw only a handful of her poems published during her life, today she is recognized as an innovator whose writing was ahead of its time.

The daughter of a lawyer-turned-politician, Dickinson grew up in a prominent household in Amherst, Massachusetts. She attended grammar school and spent a year as a boarding student at Mount Holyoke Female Seminary. While there, in an early show of her rebellious nature, when all students who wanted to be Christians were asked to rise, only Dickinson remained seated—leading the school to classify her as "without hope."

Dickinson had little interest in marriage, and lived her life in the family home, ensconced in her bedroom. She nurtured a close—probably romantic—relationship with her sister-in-law, Susan, who was also the first reader of most of her poetry. She eventually withdrew from social life entirely, living via her writing. Seven poems were published while she was alive, but she bound nearly 2,000 into "fascicles" (similar to chapbooks), which were discovered after her death and released posthumously.

Dickinson's poetry didn't follow the expected forms of the time; she used irregular meter and unconventional punctuation, and often wrote about death, life, nature, and identity. When her first collection was published, it was heavily edited to smooth out her eccentricities (as well as to omit numerous mentions of the name "Susan"). And while, by the 1920s, her work found a cult following for its exciting modernity, it wasn't until a revised 1998 publication that it was restored to its original daring punctuation and form.

Today, Dickinson is one of the most revered American writers, and her work and life have inspired numerous adaptations and tributes. Her cocktail takes a floral theme, as she was a passionate gardener who loved flowers and sometimes used the nickname Daisy.

Amanda Gorman

The Amanda Gorman

1½ shots white rum
¾ shot Lillet Blanc
½ shot blue curaçao
½ shot fresh lime juice
<u>Garnish</u>: lime rind

Add all ingredients to a shaker filled with ice. Shake vigorously and fine strain into a Nick and Nora glass. Garnish with lime rind twisted on a gold cocktail pick.

Amanda Gorman made history as the youngest ever poet to perform at a US inauguration. And if the writer and orator has her way, one day she'll be President, too.

Gorman grew up in Los Angeles, the daughter of a single mother who was an English teacher. Her mom encouraged her love of words, and as a child, Gorman began to write poetry. Because of an auditory processing disorder and speech impediment that made mastering pronunciation more difficult, she focused on reading and writing—and came to see her impediments as a strength that helped her talents flourish. While in high school, reading the work of poets like Audre Lorde expanded Gorman's worldview, and her poetry became more activist, themed around social justice, race, and feminism.

Inspired by Malala Yousafzai, Gorman became a youth delegate for the UN in 2013. In 2014, she became the first youth poet laureate of Los Angeles, publishing her first book of poetry, *The One for Whom Food Is Not Enough*, a year later. While she was attending Harvard University in 2017, she was selected as the first National Youth Poet Laureate. From there, her star rose further, and in 2020, she graduated cum laude and appeared on John Krasinki's TV show to deliver a virtual commencement speech for all those who couldn't attend their graduations due to the pandemic.

When Gorman read her poem "The Hill We Climb" at the inauguration of Joe Biden in January 2020, she addressed an American populace rocked by the attack on their capitol earlier that month. Her words confronted the political situation head-on, striving to provide a message of unity. When the book version of her poem was published in March 2021 (with a foreword by Oprah), it was an immediate bestseller, followed later that year by *Call Us What We Carry: Poems*, another bestseller that was praised for being a beacon of hope through the social unrest and isolation of the Covid era.

Gorman has often said that she aspires to become President in 2036—a goal that, given all she's achieved up to this point, seems entirely possible. The drink dedicated to her is a riff on a classic El Presidente cocktail that's the same vivid blue as the cover of her book.

Mary *Oliver*

The Mary Oliver**

2	shots Seedlip Garden
¾	shot basic simple syrup (p. 142)
¾	shot fresh lime juice
1	2-inch (5-cm) piece of cucumber, peeled and diced
4	mint leaves

Garnish: bunch of mint and edible wildflowers

Add all ingredients to a shaker. Muddle mint and cucumber. Add ice, shake vigorously, and strain into a rocks glass over an ice globe. Garnish.

** This is a zero-proof cocktail.

Mary Oliver's love for the natural world inspired emotionally resonant verses that made her one of the most popular poets of the 20th century.

She grew up in pastoral surroundings in a semirural suburb outside of Cleveland, Ohio. Oliver's childhood wasn't happy; neglect and abuse caused her to seek escape in writing, creating her own imaginary world in words. She spent a great deal of time outside, walking— a habit that lasted her whole life.

Leaving home as a teenager, Oliver traveled to Steepletop in upstate New York, the former home of the poet Edna St. Vincent Millay, and befriended Millay's sister. Oliver lived there for several years, helping organize the Pulitzer Prize-winning poet's papers. In the late 1950s she visited Steepletop again, and met the photographer Molly Malone Cook, who became her lifelong romantic partner and literary agent.

Oliver published her first collection in 1963, when she was 28. For her fifth volume, 1984's *American Primitive*, she won the Pulitzer Prize for Poetry. She was prolific, and released new work every year or two. By 2007, the *New York Times* had deemed her "far and away, this country's best-selling poet." Oliver's poetry was written in an intimate, unadorned style that spoke directly to readers. She was often inspired by long walks in nature, on which she would carry a small, hand-sewn notebook to record ideas while she strolled. Images from the wild pervade her writing: the moonlit sea, grasshoppers, wild geese. Her turns of phrase are so evocative and persevering that they have wound their way into the popular culture: if you ever consider the needs of the "soft animal" of your body, or contemplate plans for your "one wild and precious life," those are poignant words from Oliver's two most famous poems, "Wild Geese" and "The Summer Day."

The cocktail dedicated to her tastes like verdant nature, and is garnished with a wild bouquet.

82

Rupi Kaur

The Rupi Kaur

```
2    shots gin
1    shot fresh lemon juice
½    shot yellow Chartreuse
½    shot honey syrup
     (p. 143)
```
<u>Garnish</u>: 2 small sunflowers

Add all ingredients to
a shaker filled with ice.
Shake vigorously and fine
strain into a coupe glass.
Garnish.

Rupi Kaur transformed poetry from a quiet, outside-the-mainstream discipline into a pop culture phenomenon that can pack theaters with thousands of fans.

Growing up in Canada as a shy child and speaking English as a second language, the India-born Kaur had a hard time making friends. However, she eventually found companionship in reading books, and made the local library her hangout. Discovering poetry gave her a voice, and she began performing spoken word as a teenager. Kaur also started to post unpunctuated lowercase verse, inspired by Sikh scripture and poets like Kahlil Gibran and Sharon Olds, at first on Tumblr, and later on Instagram. Addressing emotionally raw topics such as trauma and abuse, self-care, acceptance, and healing, her delicately illustrated verses attracted thousands of followers.

When Kaur was in university studying rhetoric and professional writing, she self-published a collection titled *Milk and Honey*, selling 10,000 copies. But after Instagram censored a photo she posted of herself wearing gray sweatpants stained with period blood, she became a viral sensation known for fighting against the policing of women's bodies. The attention landed her a book deal with a major publisher, and *Milk and Honey* remained on the *New York Times* bestsellers list for nearly a year, selling millions of copies worldwide. Kaur's second book, *The Sun and Her Flowers*, is a deeper, more emotional volume divided into sections reflecting the life cycle of a flower, while her third book, *Home Body*, touches on the past, present, and future of the self. And 2022's *Healing Through Words* helps readers channel Kaur by exploring their identity through guided writing exercises.

As an "Instapoet" who crafts simple verse that taps into readers' emotions and who leverages social media to find her audience, Kaur is undeniably modern, and unlike most poets, she's ascended to mainstream celebrity. Reflecting her generational importance to Millennial readers, she was deemed "Writer of the Decade" by *The New Republic*.

The cocktail dedicated to Kaur is a sunny yellow, and finds its sweetness from a touch of honey.

1934
–
1992

Audre Lorde

The Audre Lorde

1½ shots avocado tequila
     (p. 143)
¾   shot non-alcoholic
     falernum
¾   shot fresh lime juice
¼   shot basic simple syrup
     (p. 142)
<u>Garnish</u>: nasturtium flowers
and leaves

Add all ingredients to
a shaker filled with ice.
Shake vigorously, strain
into a rocks glass filled
with ice, and garnish.

Audre Lorde knew who she was, and declared it thus: "Black, lesbian, mother, warrior, poet."

The child of Caribbean immigrants, Lorde grew up in New York City. She was legally blind as a kid, but taught herself to read when she was four and became infatuated with poetry. While she was attending a high school for gifted students, her school's literary journal rejected a poem she wrote for being inappropriate; Lorde submitted that same poem to *Seventeen* magazine, who published it. She later attended college in Mexico and at Hunter College in New York, and immersed herself in Greenwich Village's gay culture. She became a librarian and also a college teacher, and her involvement with academia influenced her writing.

Lorde's poetry advocated for social justice and depicted queer sexuality. Her first volume, *The First Cities*, was published in 1968; her third, *From a Land Where Other People Live*, was nominated for a National Book Award. But it was her 1976 collection, *Coal*, that broke her into the mainstream and established her as a name within the Black Arts Movement. Lorde is equally known for her essays; 1977's "The Transformation of Silence into Language and Action" positioned silence in the face of injustice as a form of violence. A line from that essay is often quoted today: "Your silence will not protect you." Her influential 1984 collection, *Sister Outsider*, brought together her prose works beginning from 1976, exploring intersectionality, sexism, racism, and ageism.

Lorde ranged into memoir, too. She was diagnosed with breast cancer in 1978 and had a mastectomy. In response, she wrote *The Cancer Journals*, a ahead-of-its-time memoir of women's pain and healing. And in 1982, she published *Zami: A New Spelling of My Name*, a memoir that delved into her inner life and erotic awareness. From 1991 until her death the following year, Lorde was New York State's poet laureate.

Her cocktail involves avocados, a fruit she imagines using with a lover in great sensual detail in *Zami*.

Genre
Fiction

Genre fiction didn't get the respect it deserved for many years—science fiction, fantasy, horror, mystery, thrillers, romance, and erotica were designated as less serious subtypes of fiction, outside the realm of the literary. But because of that divide, genre fiction developed its own passionate fanbase and its own awards, and became a thriving literary sub-world where writers are free to experiment.

Genre fiction was arguably started by women, and many of its most famous authors are female. Mary Shelley's *Frankenstein*, about a scientist who reanimates a corpse, is recognized as the first work of science fiction. And while sci-fi became a white-male-dominated genre in the first half of the 20th century, prominent writers like Ursula K. Le Guin and Octavia E. Butler reshaped the field to integrate the experiences of women and people of color—and in the process, brought the field more widespread recognition, and paved the way for future experimentation by authors like the wildly creative Carmen Maria Machado. Agatha Christie—the world's bestselling author after Shakespeare—is synonymous with mystery, while Gillian Flynn turned thrillers and horror on their head by re-envisioning the face of evil as female.

These wide-open and imaginative worlds created by women offer plenty of inspiration for cocktails—especially ones with a subversive flair.

Mary Shelley

The Mary Shelley

1½ shots amber tequila
1   shot sweet vermouth
¾   shot fresh lime juice
½   shot Cherry Heering
2   dashes Angostura bitters
Garnish: brandied cherry

Add all ingredients to
a shaker filled with ice.
Shake vigorously and strain
into a cocktail glass.
Garnish with a brandied
cherry on a cocktail pick.

Mary Shelley's *Frankenstein* helped a modernizing world confront the moral complexities of technology. While that book—credited as the first major work of science fiction—looms over her legacy, she's finally today recognized as one of the major Romantic literary figures.

Shelley was born in London into literary credentials: her mother was Mary Wollstonecraft, the trailblazing feminist philosopher who wrote *A Vindication of the Rights of Woman*, while her father, William Godwin, was a radical political philosopher. Wollstonecraft died from complications due to childbirth, so Shelley was raised by her father. As was common for girls at the time, she received no formal education. However, she had access to her father's library, was tutored, and briefly attended a boarding school. When she was still only 16, she fell in love and eloped with one of her father's literary associates, the Romantic poet Percy Bysshe Shelley.

Two years later, the two traveled to Geneva to spend the summer at the poet Lord Byron's villa. One evening while sitting around a fire, Byron suggested everyone there might write a ghost story. Shelley soon became gripped by the idea of a reanimated corpse, which ended up being the core of her novel, *Frankenstein; or, The Modern Prometheus*, which was published when she was only 20. It tells the tale of a scientist (Victor Frankenstein) who creates a sentient creature from reanimated parts gathered from "the dissecting room and the slaughter-house." The novel was a huge success, but not everyone appreciated the brilliance of its author, with some suggesting that perhaps Percy Shelley really wrote the book. Still, into her forties and after her husband's death, Shelley continued to support her family through her writing. Today, her greatest creation, *Frankenstein*, continues to inspire imitations and adaptations with its originality and persevering relevance.

The cocktail inspired by Shelley also combines elements from different places and reanimates them in a new creation. Part Manhattan, part Margarita, it's a unique creature.

Octavia E. Butler

The Octavia E. Butler

```
2    shots bourbon
1    shot tawny port
3    dashes Angostura
     bitters
```
Garnish: lemon peel

Pour bourbon and port into a mixing glass, and add bitters. Add ice and stir with a bar spoon for about 20 seconds. Strain into a coupe glass and garnish with a thick-cut piece of lemon peel.

An innovative writer of speculative fiction, Octavia E. Butler expanded the boundaries of sci-fi to include the experiences of marginalized communities—especially Black women, who were often her protagonists.

As a child growing up in Pasadena, California, Butler was extremely shy and considered herself "ugly and stupid, clumsy, and socially hopeless." But she took refuge in the library, immersing herself in science fiction magazines. At the time, the genre was dominated by white men who populated their worlds with people like themselves. Butler decided to change things when she began to craft her own stories: "I wrote myself in, since I'm me and I'm here and I'm writing," she told the *New York Times*.

Butler worked for years to find success. Rather than pursuing a traditional career, she took on temp jobs that gave her the flexibility to work on her writing in the early morning. And in the late 1970s, after publishing the first three books in her Patternist series, she was finally able to live off her writing.

Today, Butler is most famous for her restrained prose describing bleak landscapes where survivors are central to the narrative. In 1984 and 1985, she won prestigious Hugo awards for her stories "Speech Sounds," about a pandemic that causes people to lose the ability to communicate, and "Bloodchild," which depicts a colony of humans who carry the eggs of aliens. In 1995, she became the first science fiction writer to ever win a MacArthur "Genius Grant." Her best-known novel remains *Kindred*, the story of a Black woman who time-travels to the pre-Civil War South to save the life of a white enslaver who also happens to be her ancestor, and whose survival is necessary for her own.

Butler's strong, spare writing style deserves an uncompromising, stripped-down cocktail; this one plays with the traditional Manhattan formula by introducing an outsider ingredient: port.

Carmen Maria Machado

The Carmen Maria Machado

```
1    shot gin
1    shot Mirto
1    shot triple sec
1    shot fresh lemon juice
1    dash absinthe
```
Garnish: white orchid

Add all ingredients to
a shaker filled with ice.
Shake vigorously, fine
strain into a coupe glass,
and garnish.

Carmen Maria Machado's sensual, vivid writing harnesses the imaginative power of horror, fantasy, and other genres to explore the way women—especially queer women—experience the world.

As a child growing up in Allentown, Pennsylvania, Machado learned storytelling through the oral tradition of her part-Cuban family, and began writing while very young—even submitting a chapter of a novel to Scholastic after finding their address in the back of a Baby-Sitters Club book. But while she was always an author at heart, she experimented with schooling in journalism, and then photography, before pursuing storytelling in earnest. While completing her MFA at the Iowa Writers' Workshop, Machado began reading genre fiction, including work by the acclaimed horror and mystery writer Shirley Jackson, and started to pen her own surreal works that foregrounded queerness, sex, and gender.

She went on to publish *Her Body and Other Parties* in 2017, a short story collection that took her five years to write (while working at a bath products store). Over the course of eight stories, Machado uses the trappings of horror, sci-fi, fairy tales, and *Law & Order: SVU* to conjure the strange reality of being a woman. The success of that book—which won the Shirley Jackson Award, was a finalist for the National Book Award, and featured a story nominated for a Nebula Award—gave her the freedom to write an even more experimental second book. Published in 2019, *In the Dream House* is Machado's shapeshifting memoir of an abusive relationship with a woman, as told through brief chapters that examine the narrative through different lenses or tropes ("Dream House as Unreliable Narrator"; "Dream House as Noir"; and so on). Praised for its intoxicating-yet-horrifying style, the book proved Machado to be a nimble, risk-taking writer capable of rendering any topic beautifully on the page.

Her cocktail is blood red and a little bewitching, utilizing the cult-favorite myrtle berry liqueur, Mirto.

Agatha Christie

The Agatha Christie

1½   shots vodka
½   shot crème de menthe
½   shot crème de cacao
1   shot fresh lemon juice
1   egg white
Garnish: chocolate truffle

Add all ingredients to a shaker without ice and dry shake. Add ice, shake vigorously, and strain into a Nick and Nora glass. Garnish with a chocolate truffle on a cocktail pick.

A bestselling novelist outsold only by Shakespeare and the Bible, Agatha Christie perfected the mystery format and shaped the idea that the solution to a crime is often right in front of our eyes.

Christie grew up in a wealthy home in the seaside town of Torquay, England. As a child she wrote and performed plays, and when she was convalescing from illness at age 18, she penned her first short story. The first novel she wrote was rejected by publishers, but that didn't stop her. During the First and Second World Wars, she worked in hospital pharmacies, where she learned about poisons—knowledge she would apply to her murder mysteries.

Christie finally published a novel, *The Mysterious Affair at Styles*, in 1920, introducing the world to Hercule Poirot, a mustachioed Belgian detective who would appear in 33 of her books. In 1930, she debuted another famous character in *The Murder at the Vicarage*: Miss Marple, an elderly spinster who also happens to be an ace amateur sleuth. In 1939, she published what many consider to be her best novel: *And Then There Were None*. A "locked room" mystery, it tells the story of eight people invited to an island by a mysterious stranger, who are then picked off, one by one.

Several of Christie's novels have been adapted into films—one example is *Murder on the Orient Express*, directed in 1974 by Sidney Lumet and in 2017 by Kenneth Branagh. Christie's stage play *The Mousetrap*, which debuted in London in 1952, is also the world's longest-running play; its run was only disrupted in 2020 by the coronavirus pandemic.

Fans of Christie's work love the complex puzzles of her plots, layered with clues and red herrings. Some readers like to try to solve the mystery themselves; others like to sit back and let Miss Marple or Poirot do the work. The cocktail dedicated to Christie is based on one of the iconoclastic Poirot's favorite tipples: crème de menthe.

Ursula K. Le Guin

The Ursula K. Le Guin

1   lime-mint ice globe
     (p. 144)
2   shots white rum
¾   shot basic simple
     syrup (p. 142)
¾   shot fresh lime juice
4   blackberries

Place lime-mint ice
globe in a rocks glass.
Add rum, basic simple
syrup, lime juice, and
blackberries to a shaker.
Muddle blackberries.
Add ice, shake, and fine
strain over ice globe.

Ursula K. Le Guin imagined worlds beyond our own—and different ways of being.

She grew up in Berkeley, California, the youngest of four children. Her father was an anthropologist and her mother a writer, and as a child, Le Guin took advantage of the family's book collection. In particular, she delved into mythology and comparative religion, such as James Frazer's *The Golden Bough*, and also the *Tao Te Ching*, which influenced her later work. In college, she studied romance literature, earning a master's from Columbia, and won a Fulbright scholarship to study in Paris. There, she met her husband, and quit academia to raise a family and pursue writing.

Le Guin chose to write science fiction because, as a genre less scrutinized than literary fiction, it allowed her freedom to experiment. At first, she catered to the conventions of the genre, writing male heroes—but later, she asserted her feminism and began centering female protagonists.

Her second published book, 1968's *A Wizard of Earthsea*, brought her widespread fame. A fantasy novel targeted at young adults, it was set in a fictional oceanic world where some people wield magic, a force in which they must find balance.

One of Le Guin's most provocative novels, 1969's *The Left Hand of Darkness*, explored a world where there is no gender—Le Guin said she "eliminated gender, to find out what was left"—and it won both the Hugo Award and the Nebula. And 1974's *The Dispossessed*, a work of anarchist utopian science fiction, was set on twin planets, one capitalist and the other classless and utopian. It too won the Hugo and the Nebula.

Over her more than 20 novels, Le Guin helped establish science fiction and fantasy as genres worthy of literary respect. In her 2014 speech on receiving the Medal for Distinguished Contribution to American Letters, she memorably described writers like her as "realists of a larger reality."

Le Guin's cocktail includes an otherworldly ice globe flavored with mint (and possibility).

Gillian Flynn

The Gillian Flynn

2   shots bourbon
1   tray blood orange
    ice cubes (p. 143)
<u>Garnish</u>: half a blood
orange wheel

Add bourbon, blood orange
ice cubes, and one regular
ice cube to a shaker.
Shake until ice is
pulverized, strain into
a Nick and Nora glass,
and garnish.

In the literary world of Gillian Flynn, women and girls are wily and dangerous—equally likely to be villains or heroines.

Though she writes dark thrillers, Flynn's childhood was happy and ordinary. She grew up in Kansas City, Missouri, the daughter of two community college professors who taught reading and film—and thus, Flynn was surrounded by books and movies. She studied English and journalism at the University of Kansas, and later, got her master's in journalism from Northwestern. She wanted to be a crime reporter, but was too shy to interview people at the scene. Instead, she put her childhood immersion in film to good use and moved to New York to work as a reporter for *Entertainment Weekly* magazine.

While at the magazine, Flynn began writing novels on the side. Her debut, *Sharp Objects*, is a mystery about a journalist who returns to her Missouri hometown to investigate a series of murders, and uncovers terrifying family secrets. Her follow-up, *Dark Places*, features a bitter, cynical young woman who survived what seemed to be a Satanic mass murder and, years later, falls in with a group of amateur investigators who motivate her to find the truth. It became a *New York Times* bestseller.

The book that changed everything, though, was *Gone Girl*. Alternating between the perspectives of a married couple, Nick and Amy Dunne, it unravels the mystery of Amy's disappearance, building tension through unreliable narration. A massive hit, *Gone Girl* sold millions of copies and earned Flynn comparisons to acclaimed thriller writer Patricia Highsmith. It was later adapted into a film, directed by David Fincher; adaptations of *Dark Places* and *Sharp Objects* soon followed.

Flynn's female characters are known for being dysfunctional and a bit wild. *Gone Girl*'s success sparked a wave of thrillers and mysteries about similarly complicated women, a trend the *Guardian* deemed "the *Gone Girl* effect."

Flynn's cocktail is a little bloody, and ice cold.

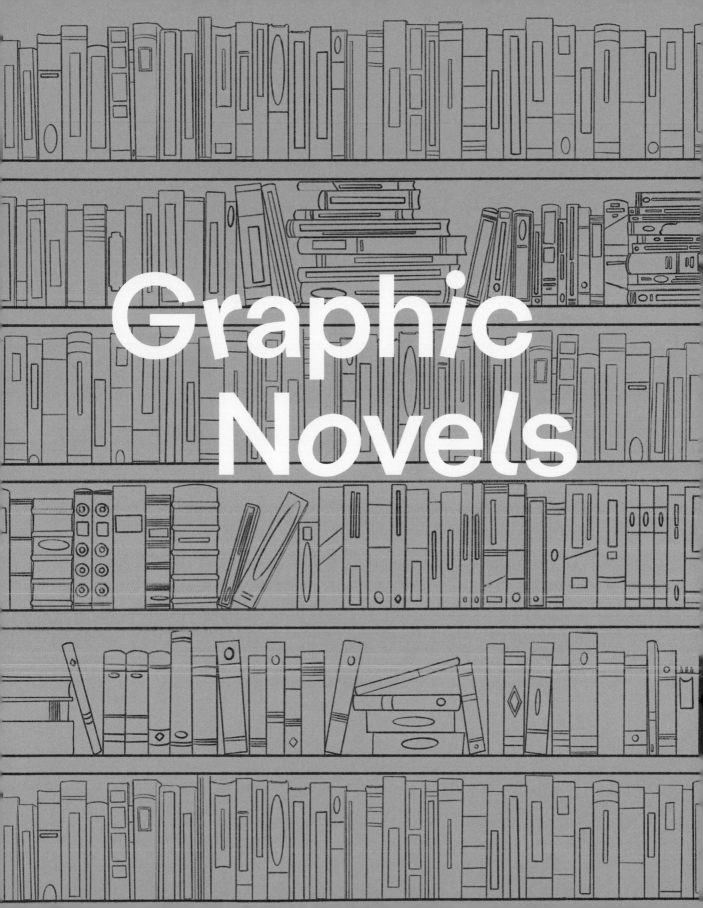

Graphic
Novels

106

Graphic novels use art to tell a story, and that story can be any variety of fiction or nonfiction. While they're more a format than a genre, graphic novels have their own distinct space within literary culture.

Graphic novels sprang from the world of comics, serialized illustrated strips that appeared in the back of newspapers beginning in the late 19th century. Longer and more serious than most comics, and aimed at an adult audience, graphic novels emerged in the late 1970s and '80s and used illustration to tell the same types of complex, longform stories told in novels and nonfiction books. In particular, Art Spiegelman's *Maus*, a 1986 graphic novel about the Holocaust which won the Pulitzer, brought new recognition to the genre.

Comics have often been seen as a male-dominated field, but women creators and readers have been a force in graphic novels since the beginning, and graphic novels by women are some of the best known and most popular. Marjane Satrapi's *Persepolis* and Alison Bechdel's *Fun Home*, both graphic memoirs, are two modern classics with huge influence. Since graphic novels are a relatively new phenomenon, this section of the book is the smallest—but the writers in it are setting a path for generations of graphic novelists to come. That, of course, deserves a toast.

Marjane Satrapi

The Marjane Satrapi

2   shots gin
¾   shot spiced plum syrup
       (p. 143)
¾   shot fresh lemon juice
1   shot aquafaba
<u>Garnish</u>: dried edible
flowers

Add all ingredients to
a shaker filled with ice.
Shake vigorously and
strain into a Nick and Nora
glass. Garnish with dried
edible flowers sprinkled
elegantly across one side
of the foam.

With her bold black-and-white comics exploring life during and after the Islamic Revolution in Iran, Marjane Satrapi has made an indelible mark on the canon of graphic novels, earning a reputation as one of the most important contemporary graphic memoirists.

Satrapi was raised in a middle-class home in Tehran, the child of liberal-minded parents. As a young girl in 1980, a year after the revolution toppled the Shah, she witnessed how growing religious extremism after Iran became an Islamic republic sapped the rights of citizens, especially women. Following the execution of her communist uncle and a bombing on her street, Satrapi's parents sent her away to the safety of Austria. She tells this harrowing story in her groundbreaking graphic novel, *Persepolis: The Story of a Childhood*, which was translated into multiple languages, sold around the world, and eventually adapted into an Oscar-nominated film, making Satrapi—now a resident of Paris—a household name.

Prior to her success, the world of graphic novels was largely considered a male domain. Rejecting the idea that comics were for men, Satrapi used black-and-white illustrations to tell her life story because, as she told the *Guardian*, "I always thought that what I had to say was too much; it was complicated with lots and lots of words." Choosing the visual language of comics allowed her to transcend borders and tell a complex story in an immediately understandable, powerful way.

Persepolis's massive popularity demanded a sequel, and Satrapi's follow-up, *Persepolis: The Story of a Return*, detailed her difficult teenage years in Austria and her return to Iran. Following that, she published two other graphic novels: *Embroideries*, about the sex lives of Iranian women, and *Chicken with Plums*, about her musician great-uncle. While Satrapi's creative output these days is largely as a film writer and director, her influence on graphic novels is undeniable, with *Persepolis* acknowledged as a modern classic.

Her cocktail involves plums, with some added spice.

Alison Bechdel

The Alison Bechdel

1½ shots Scotch
1   shot fresh pink
     grapefruit juice
½   shot basic simple
     syrup (p. 142)
2   1-inch (2.5-cm) chunks
     of mango
1   dried chili
Garnish: grapefruit twist

Add all ingredients to
a shaker, and muddle mango
and chili with liquid.
Add ice, shake vigorously,
fine strain into a coupe
glass, and garnish.

Graphic memoirist Alison Bechdel has changed the way we look at stories about women, and carved a space for lesbian representation within mainstream comic-strip culture.

Growing up in Pennsylvania, Bechdel was a tomboy, keeping her hair short and playing with the neighborhood boys. She began to draw when she was three years old, and as she grew older, realized she was mostly drawing men because she had absorbed that they were always the central figure in a story. She only drew women later, as she became comfortable with her lesbian identity while studying at Oberlin College.

After moving to Manhattan and working office jobs in the publishing industry, Bechdel began writing a comic strip called *Dykes to Watch Out For*, one of the earliest pop culture depictions of lesbians. In 1985, Bechdel published a strip of *DTWOF* called "The Rule" in which a character states that she'll only go see a movie if: 1) the movie has at least two women in it; 2) the two women talk to each other; 3) their conversation is about something other than a man. Known today as the Bechdel Test, it's a widely cited barometer for female representation in film—and only about 50 per cent of films pass it.

Fun Home, Bechdel's first graphic novel memoir, pushed her from indie credibility to mainstream success. Published in 2006, it chronicles her own coming out and relationship with her dad, a closeted gay man. Hailed as one of the best books of the year, it helped cement the status of graphic novels as real literature and was later adapted into a Broadway musical. She followed that with two other graphic memoirs: *Are You My Mother?*, which explores her troubled relationship with her emotionally distant mom, and *The Secret to Superhuman Strength*, about her lifelong pursuit of exercise.

One of *DTWOF*'s characters, Sydney, is a fan of Loch Lomond Scotch; this cocktail considers Scotch from a new perspective.

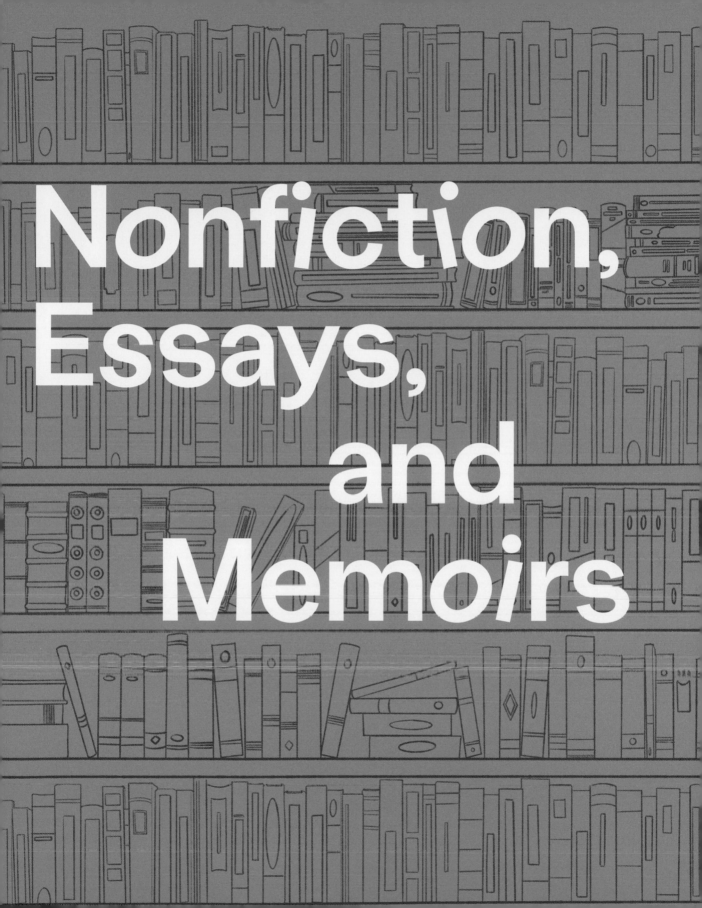

Nonfiction, Essays, and Memoirs

114

Nonfiction is a broad category containing
many subgenres, but essays and memoirs are
among the most popular. By their nature, essays
and memoirs incorporate a writer's personal
perspective and experience, and the lives
of women over time and the specific concerns
of the eras they lived in have shaped the
writing they produce.

The authors in this section range from
Simone de Beauvoir, who wrote the essential
pre-second-wave feminist book of philosophy,
The Second Sex, in 1949, which argues that
gender was imposed on women, to Susan Sontag,
whose mid-century essays focus on aesthetics
and meaning; from Angela Davis, whose activism
led to a memoir that argues for prison
abolition, to Roxane Gay, who has shaped
the modern discourse about imperfect feminism
and body size; from Joan Didion, who wrote
incisively and evocatively about everything
from counterculture Los Angeles to grief,
to Jia Tolentino, who perfectly encapsulates
what it means to exist in a reality warped
by the internet. Wherever you start, the
writers here have distinct voices and brilliant
insights that will change the way you look at
the world—and make you want to raise a glass
in their honor.

Jia Tolentino

The Jia Tolentino

1½ shots gin
¾   shot butterfly pea
     flower syrup (p. 142)
¾   shot fresh lemon and
     lime juice (mix half-
     and-half)
1   bar spoon maraschino
     liqueur
3   shots club soda
     (soda water)
Garnish: mint

Add all ingredients except
club soda to a shaker
filled with ice. Shake
vigorously and strain into
a Collins glass full of
ice. Top with club soda,
gently stir, garnish, and
serve with a steel straw.

It's easy to get lost in the warped funhouse of
contemporary culture, but luckily for us, clear-eyed
Jia Tolentino can see her way through. The essayist,
heralded as the voice of the Millennial generation, uses
her writing to illuminate how we live today—and how we
commodify ourselves in the process.

Tolentino's childhood influences gave her the
perfect background for understanding late-capitalist
American reality. Born in Toronto, she grew up in an
evangelical megachurch community in Houston, Texas. As
a teen she was a cheerleader, and appeared on a reality
television show called *Girls v. Boys*. She eagerly
participated in the early internet, creating detailed
personal webpages with HTML. She later attended the
traditionalist University of Virginia, and afterwards,
served in the Peace Corps in Kyrgyzstan. Eventually, she
got her MFA from the University of Michigan.

Tolentino's first notable bylines appeared on
women's website The Hairpin, followed by Gawker-
associated feminist website Jezebel in 2014. She joined
The New Yorker in 2016, for whom she began to pen essays
about online culture, literature, music, and feminism,
raising the magazine's profile among a younger, more
online demographic in the process. And in 2019 she
published *Trick Mirror*, a bestselling essay collection
that captured the zeitgeist and earned her comparisons
to Joan Didion for her perceptive, nuanced way of
looking at our world.

One of Tolentino's best-known essays, published
in *Trick Mirror*, is "Ecstasy," in which she writes
about both her formative years in Houston, and the way
drugs and religion tap into the same human desire
for transcendence. The cocktail dedicated to her takes
inspiration from lean, a purple beverage invented
in Houston that helped shape the sound of chopped
and screwed rap, the woozy soundtrack to Tolentino's
younger years.

Eve Babitz

1943
–
2021

The Eve Babitz

2   shots watermelon rum
      (p. 144)
½   shot fresh lime juice
½   shot basic simple
      syrup (p. 142)
2   shots rosé champagne
<u>Garnish</u>: mint

In a shaker with ice,
shake watermelon rum, lime
juice, and basic simple
syrup. Fine strain into a
coupe glass, top with rosé
champagne, and garnish.

Eve Babitz embodied hedonism both in writing and in life. In her personal essays and novels, she epitomized the sensual joys and excesses of Los Angeles.

Babitz was raised in LA in a creative, free-wheeling family: her mother was an artist, and her father was a violinist; her godfather was the composer Igor Stravinsky. At Hollywood High, she smoked, drank, and read novels rather than studying. She wrote of her teenage sexual awakening, "I got deflowered on two cans of Rainier Ale when I was 17." She became famous at age 20 when she posed naked for a photo, playing chess with Marcel Duchamp—all to get revenge on the gallerist she was having an affair with.

Babitz was a sexually assertive, extravagant consumer of liquor and drugs, known for her relationships with famous men like Jim Morrison (who wrote "L.A. Woman" about her), Ed Ruscha (who included her in his work *Five 1965 Girlfriends*), Steve Martin, and Harrison Ford. Babitz documented her exploits with zeal, making her literary debut at age 28 with 1972's memoir essay collection *Eve's Hollywood*, which featured an Annie Leibovitz-shot photo of Babitz on its cover in a bikini and feather boa. Another Babitz classic, 1979's *Sex and Rage: Advice to Young Ladies Eager for a Good Time*, an autobiographical novel, follows a party girl named Jacaranda as she imbibes cocktail upon cocktail and eventually abandons Los Angeles for New York.

Later, Babitz quit her habit of partying at the Chateau Marmont, but her bon vivant lifestyle from the 1960s through '80s remains her signature. While she didn't initially achieve the same level of success as Joan Didion (to whom her work is often compared), she's been rediscovered and exalted by contemporary readers. Several of her books have been reissued, including *Sex and Rage*, which became a bestseller in 2017, 38 years after it was originally published.

Babitz's cocktail is sultry, decadent, and guaranteed to get you on her level.

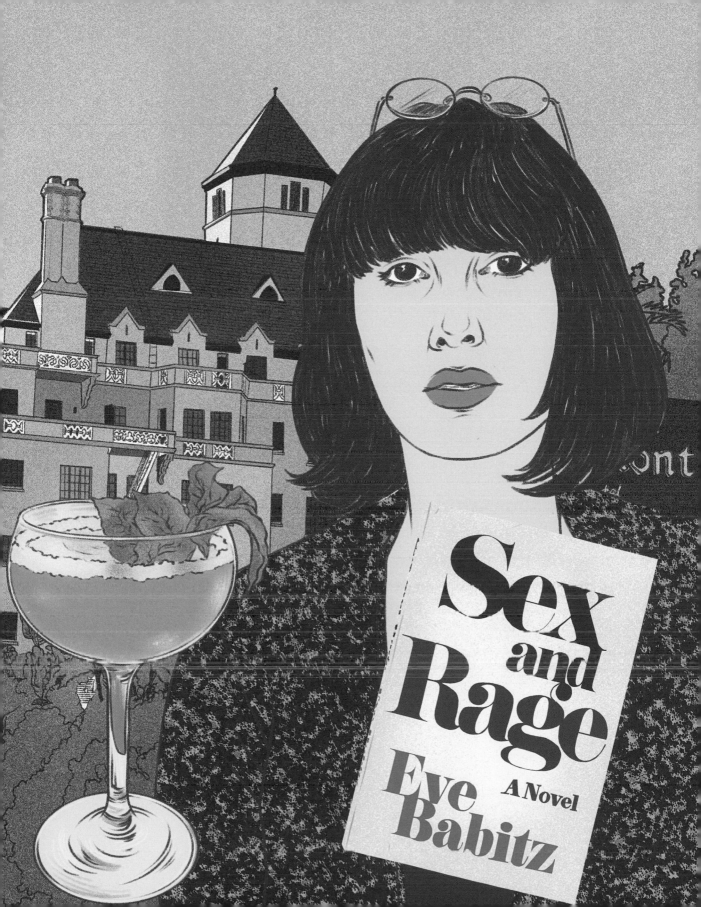

bell hooks

The bell hooks

4   shots hot lemon
      ginger tea
1   shot gin
1   shot Campari
1   shot vermouth
Garnish: orange wheel

Steep tea for 3 minutes
in very hot water.
In a clear mug, mix gin,
Campari, and vermouth.
Pour tea into mug, stir,
and garnish with an
orange wheel.

The inimitable thinker and author bell hooks wrote about intersectionality before it had a name and, in doing so, made space for Black and working-class women within feminism. For many, she also redefined what it means to love.

Born Gloria Jean Watkins, hooks grew up in a large, working-class family in Kentucky. As a child, she attended segregated schools, which helped shape her perspective on racial oppression. She was a bookworm, keeping her siblings up late while she read the work of William Wordsworth, Emily Dickinson, Elizabeth Barrett Browning, and other poets. While she was completing undergraduate and master's degrees in English literature (at Stanford and the University of Wisconsin, respectively), she began writing a book that she finally published in 1981. Titled *Ain't I a Woman: Black Women and Feminism* after Sojourner Truth's "Ain't I a Woman?" speech, and published under her pen name, bell hooks (a tribute to her great-grandmother, Bell Blair Hooks), the book addressed the layered effects of both racism and sexism on Black women. Groundbreaking and incendiary, it supported the arguments of Black women who didn't see their needs reflected in the male-led antiracism movement and the white-led feminist movement.

In 1983, she got her PhD (with a dissertation on Toni Morrison), which began a long career as an English professor; hooks was beloved by her students. She continued to publish widely and profusely across varying genres. While gender and race were frequent topics, she also wrote children's fiction, self-help, memoir, and poetry. When identifying their favorite works by hooks, fans often point to her books about love, especially *All About Love: New Visions*, published in 2000. It addresses how our culture undervalues love and offers solutions for how people can find transformative love based on respect, commitment, trust, and care. As she told the *New York Times* in 2015, "I believe wholeheartedly that the only way out of domination is love."

hooks's cocktail is warm and complex, much like love.

NONFICTION, ESSAYS, AND MEMOIRS

Susan Sontag

The Susan Sontag

2	shots white rum
2	shots unsweetened coconut cream
1	shot hibiscus syrup (p. 142)
1	shot fresh lime juice
4	1-inch (2.5-cm) chunks of pineapple
2	large sliced strawberries
4	large ice cubes

Garnish: hibiscus flowers, sliced strawberries, and pineapple leaves

Add all ingredients to a blender and blend until smooth. Pour into a pineapple-shaped glass, garnish, and serve with a striped paper straw.

Essayist, critic, and novelist Susan Sontag transformed aesthetics and popular culture into topics worthy of intellectual pursuit.

She was born Susan Rosenblatt in Manhattan, becoming Susan Sontag after her father passed away and her mother moved the family to Tucson and LA and remarried. Her mother was aloof and absent, and young Sontag spent her time at the library in the company of books. She graduated from high school at 16, and then attended UC Berkeley and the University of Chicago. There, at age 17, she met a professor named Philip Rieff and married him ten days later. After pursuing graduate degrees in English and philosophy and having a son with Rieff, Sontag sought a divorce and moved to New York with only a couple of suitcases. From that point on, many of her major relationships were with women, including the photographer Annie Leibovitz (to whom she was close for the last 15 years of her life).

In New York, Sontag taught at universities while writing, and in 1964, published an essay, "Notes on Camp," which immediately and irrevocably launched her into fame. It examines an aesthetic sensibility rooted in the embrace of artifice and exaggeration, which, until Sontag's essay came out, was largely only understood by the gay community. She followed that with a collection, *Against Interpretation*, the title essay of which argues that the meaning of art is less important than its visceral impact. Another essay collection, *On Photography*, won the National Book Critics Circle Award and examines how the proliferation of photography has changed society. Two later collections, *Illness as Metaphor* and *AIDS and its Metaphors*, deconstruct the language we use to discuss disease.

Sontag's essays and criticism were what brought her fame, but she found them exhausting work, sometimes taking a full year to pen a single essay. Later in her career, she refocused her attention on novels, including *The Volcano Lover* and *In America*, the latter of which was accused of plagiarism, but won the National Book Award.

The cocktail dedicated to Sontag takes its notes from camp, about which she said: "The hallmark of camp is the spirit of extravagance."

Lindy West

The Lindy West

2 shots rum
1 shot raspberry syrup
  (p. 143)
¾ shot strained fresh
  lemon juice
3 dashes Angostura
  bitters
3 shots club soda
  (soda water)
1 scoop (250 ml) vanilla
  ice cream
Garnish: lemon wheel

Add rum, syrup, lemon
juice, Angostura bitters,
and club soda to a mixing
glass and stir gently.
Scoop ice cream into
a Collins glass. Pour rum
mixture over ice cream,
garnish, and serve with
a straw.

Outspoken essayist and cultural critic Lindy West uses
humor as a tool to frame opinions on taboo topics.

West was born in Seattle, the daughter of a nurse
and a jazz pianist. Growing up, she became aware that
society considered her "too big," and shrank her persona
to compensate, becoming quiet and withdrawn for a time.
Eventually, she studied English at Occidental College
in Los Angeles, and became involved in the local comedy
scene. She was also a devotee of Howard Stern's radio
show until his misogyny turned her off. With no clear
career plan after graduating, she took an unfulfilling
job at a parenting magazine, and eventually moved back
to Seattle to work a data entry job at the city's alt
weekly, *The Stranger*.

There, West was given the opportunity to write
film reviews, and had her big break when, coming out of
her shell, she penned a scorched-earth takedown of the
film *Sex and the City 2*. While she distances herself
from the review these days (she considers it mean), it
went viral at the time, catapulting West to overnight
stardom and landing her a literary agent. The following
year, a public stand-off with *The Stranger*'s editor,
sex columnist Dan Savage, brought her more notoriety:
in response to what she viewed as fatphobic comments by
Savage, West publicly "came out" as fat with a blog post
titled "Hello, I Am Fat." It was the moment she became
an activist; she later said, "I was declaring, 'This
is who I am. I'm not going to eat shit and say thank
you anymore.'"

After her tenure at *The Stranger* ended in 2012, West
became a staff writer at feminist website Jezebel, and
contributed opinion pieces to outlets like the *Guardian*
and the *New York Times*. In 2016, she published her first
book, an essay collection titled *Shrill: Notes from a
Loud Woman*, which combined memoir and polemic on topics
such as fat acceptance, abortion stigma, and period
shame. (It was later adapted into the popular TV show
Shrill, starring Aidy Bryant.) She followed that in 2019
with *The Witches Are Coming*, another essay collection
diving into the post-#MeToo era and Trumpism, and *Shit,
Actually*, a return to the niche that brought her fame,
film reviews.

West's cocktail is brash and decadent—a drink for
someone who refuses to hide in a corner.

Simone de Beauvoir

The Simone de Beauvoir

1½ shots gin
¾ shot fresh lemon juice
¾ shot apricot syrup
    (p. 142)
2 shots champagne
<u>Garnish</u>: mint

Add gin, lemon juice, and apricot syrup to a shaker filled with ice. Shake vigorously and fine strain into a coupe glass. Top with champagne, and garnish.

Philosopher and writer Simone de Beauvoir illuminated how society defines and limits women, and, with her groundbreaking book *The Second Sex*, inspired a new wave of feminists.

Beauvoir was an intellectual little girl, and her conservative-minded father said of her, "Simone thinks like a man!" As a child she was religious, and considered becoming a nun. However, as she grew older and observed tragedies in the world, she became an atheist, believing that freedom from faith allowed her to face challenges directly and with honesty. World War I demolished her family's fortune and Beauvoir's dowry, which gave her an opportunity to make a life of her own. She studied philosophy at the Sorbonne in Paris, acquiring the equivalent of a master's degree, and started teaching and writing. She also began a romantic relationship with fellow philosopher Jean-Paul Sartre, and the two became the reigning couple of French existentialism. Their lifelong partnership was unconventional (and infamous): they never married, and pursued and shared lovers on the side.

Beauvoir was a prodigious writer, penning novels, essays, and papers on philosophy. She's best known for her feminist philosophical text *The Second Sex*, in which she famously said, "One is not born, but rather becomes, a woman." In it, she identifies how gender, constructed by a patriarchal society, imposes secondary status upon women, laying the foundation for the women's rights movement of the later 20th century. Beauvoir also had success with her novels, which were often autobiographical; for example, her 1954 Prix Goncourt-winning *roman à clef*, *The Mandarins*, follows a group of French intellectuals and philosophers that closely resembles her own social circle. She also published a popular, revealing four-volume memoir beginning with *Memoirs of a Dutiful Daughter* in 1958 and ending with *All Said and Done* in 1972.

Beauvoir enjoyed fueling philosophical debate with a cocktail; in her memoirs, she commented that she and Sartre would "drink our cocktails like connoisseurs—Bronxes, Sidecars, Bacardis, Alexanders, Martinis." However, her favorite was an apricot cocktail, a flavor shared by this drink dedicated to her.

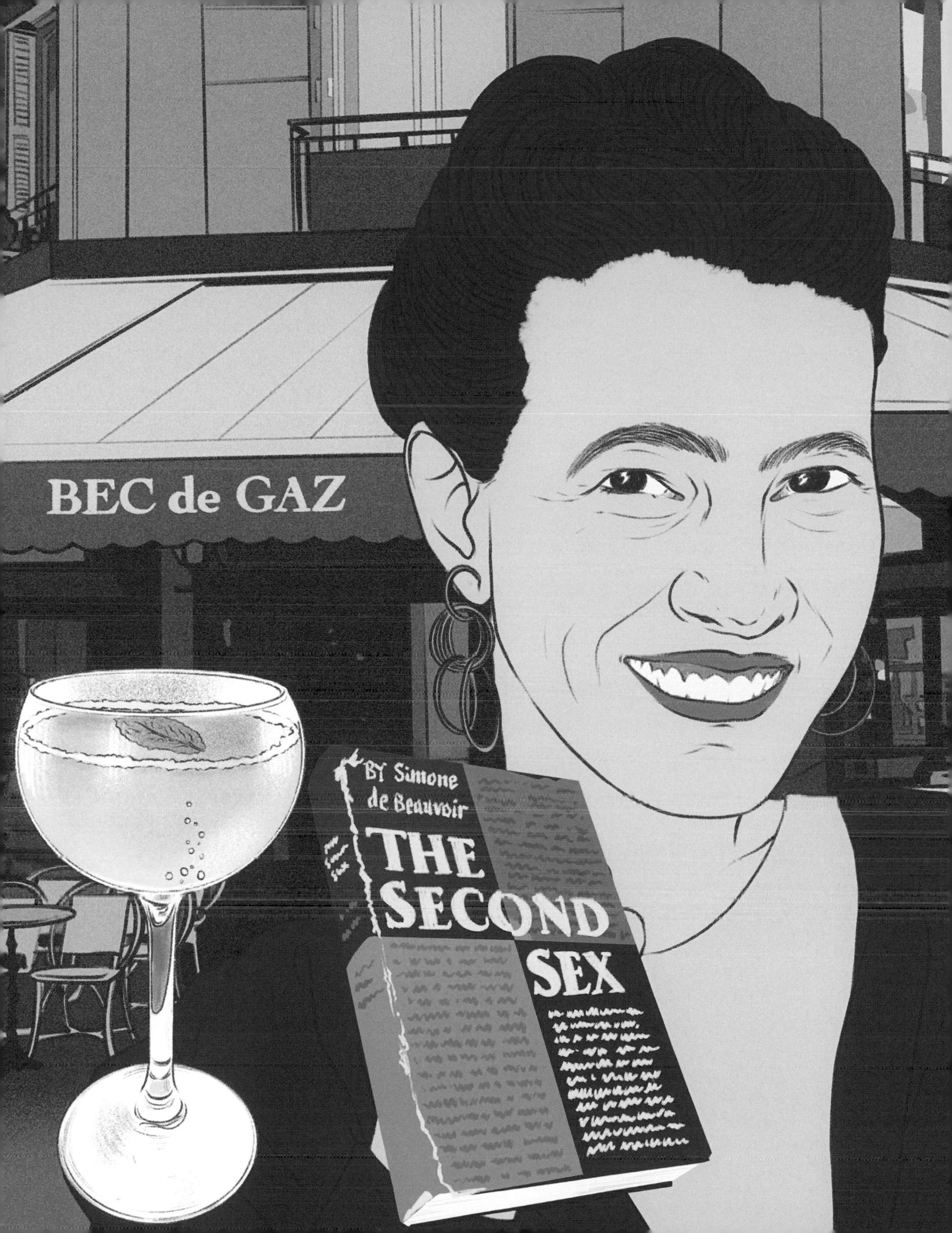
BEC de GAZ
BY Simone de Beauvoir
THE SECOND SEX

Angela Davis

The Angela Davis

1   shot ruby port
1   shot gin
¾   shot fresh lemon juice
¾   shot vanilla syrup
     (p. 143)
<u>Garnish</u>: lemon wheel

Add all ingredients to
a shaker with ice. Shake
vigorously, strain into
a rocks glass filled with
ice, and garnish.

Angela Davis writes to push for civil rights and racial justice. A lifelong activist, she is one of the enduring icons of Black political resistance.

Growing up in Birmingham, Alabama, she was surrounded by politics: her mother was an organizer for the Southern Negro Youth Congress, a Communist-affiliated organization fighting for Black liberation. Davis learned the art of protest from her time in the Girl Scouts, with whom she marched to oppose segregation.

She thrived academically; after her undergraduate at Brandeis, Davis pursued graduate school at the University of Frankfurt in Germany, where she studied under the philosopher Herbert Marcuse. Returning to the States, she became a popular philosophy and feminism professor at UCLA, known for her ties to the Communist Party and the Black Panthers. She was thrust into the national spotlight when she was charged with murder for buying weapons used by a Black teenager who kidnapped and killed a judge. She became a fugitive and was placed on the FBI's Most Wanted list; calls for her freedom became a rallying cry on the political left. After she was caught, she spent more than a year in jail before she was acquitted.

While she was in custody, Davis found a new cause: prison reform. In 1971, she edited and published an essay anthology, *If They Come in the Morning: Voices of Resistance*, about the American legal system, especially incarceration. Her first book, acquired and edited by Toni Morrison, treads similar ground. *Angela Davis: An Autobiography* tells her life story, beginning and ending with her incarceration experience, and she used the book to build a narrative around the violence of the state. She expanded on this work throughout her career; for example, with 2003's *Are Prisons Obsolete?*, which argues for the abolishment of prisons. Other favored topics include feminism (*Women, Race, and Class*) and worldwide fights for liberation (*Freedom Is a Constant Struggle*).

The Black Panthers had a signature cocktail vividly nicknamed "Panther Piss" that included port and lemon juice. Davis' cocktail incorporates those flavors, but makes them more complex.

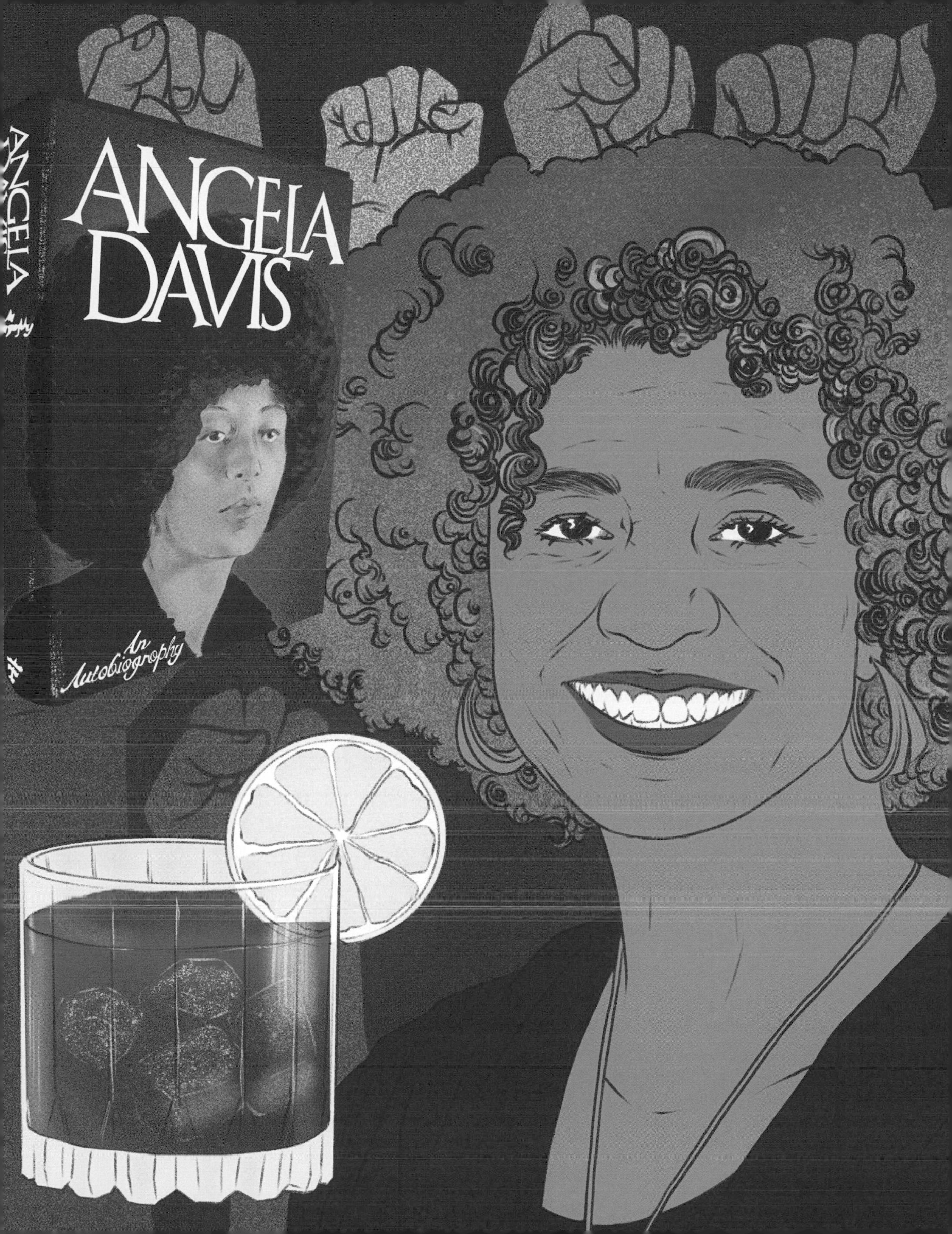
ANGELA
ANGELA DAVIS
An Autobiography

b. 1946

Patti Smith

The Patti Smith*

1 shot Pernod
½ shot basic simple
  syrup (p. 142)
½ shot fresh lemon juice
5 shots club soda
  (soda water)
<u>Garnish</u>: lemon twist

Add Pernod, basic simple
syrup, and lemon juice to
a shaker filled with ice.
Shake vigorously, strain
into a Collins glass filled
with ice, and top with club
soda. Garnish and serve
with a straw.

* This is a low-proof
cocktail.

"Punk poet" Patti Smith devotes her bohemian creativity
to both writing and performance, creating a body of
work that inspires those who like their music lyrical
and their writing unconventional.

Smith grew up in Chicago in a religious, working-
class home. As a child, she was often confined to bed
with illnesses like scarlet fever, so she entertained
herself by reading, listening to music, and dreaming
about one day creating art. After she finished school,
she began attending teacher's college while working
in a factory, and along the way, became pregnant—but,
realizing she couldn't raise a child, she gave up the
baby for adoption. Soon after, she moved to New York
with little more than a handful of essentials and
a collection of Arthur Rimbaud's poems.

On Smith's first day in New York she met Robert
Mapplethorpe, a photographer who became her lover
and creative inspiration, with whom she lived in the
dilapidated, artistic Chelsea Hotel. She wrote poems
and began performing them, eventually adding a guitarist
to her act and then an entire band, becoming associated
with the fledgling punk scene. Eventually, Smith
recorded an album titled *Horses*, which fused spoken-word
poetry with punk. A later musical collaboration with
Bruce Springsteen, the song "Because the Night," made
her a huge star.

While Smith published some collections of poetry
beginning in the 1970s (such as *Seventh Heaven* and
Babel), it wasn't until more recently that her writing
became as well known as her music. In 2010, her moving
memoir about her relationship with Mapplethorpe, *Just
Kids*, won the National Book Award. She followed that
with two other memoirs: *M Train* (about love, loss, and
creativity) and *Year of the Monkey* (about her life
during her seventieth year).

Smith adores the French poet Rimbaud, and in his
honor has sometimes quaffed Pernod, a French anise-
flavored liqueur. Her cocktail uses Pernod, and may
inspire you to write poetry.

Gloria Steinem

The Gloria Steinem

2	shots gin
¼	shot Aperol
¼	shot maraschino liqueur
½	shot fresh lemon juice
1	egg white

Garnish: brandied cherry

Add all ingredients to a shaker without ice. Dry shake, add ice, and shake until chilled. Strain into a cocktail glass and garnish with a cherry on a cocktail pick.

Journalist Gloria Steinem has been a prominent women's rights leader since the 1960s. Using her star power and skill for organizing, she expanded the audience for feminist writing.

Steinem grew up as the daughter of a traveling salesman, and her family lived on the road in a trailer. When her parents divorced, her mother was unable to hold onto a job—a situation that shaped Steinem's views that the world was opposed to working women. After she graduated from university, she had another formative experience: an abortion at age 23, during the pre-*Roe v. Wade* era when the procedure was illegal in many U.S. states.

Steinem's first major piece of journalism appeared in *Esquire* magazine; titled "The Moral Disarmament of Betty Coed," it explored the attitudes of college students towards the birth control pill. The following year, she was pushed into the spotlight by her investigative journalism piece "A Bunny's Tale," for which Steinem went undercover to work at Hugh Hefner's Playboy Club as a "Bunny" cocktail waitress to expose the venue's misogyny and borderline-illegal working conditions. That story almost ended her career; people viewed her as a Bunny rather than a writer. But she persevered, and her 1969 *New York* magazine essay "After Black Power, Women's Liberation" cemented her status as one of the leading American feminists.

Steinem cofounded the feminist magazine *Ms.* in 1972, when she was 38. The publication was immediately successful, and Steinem, as its editor, became famous. At protests and rallies for the women's movement, she was a conspicuous presence, recognized for her long, center-parted hair, aviator shades, and miniskirts.

Today, a new generation of feminists has risen, but Steinem is still extremely active in the movement. In 2015, she published her memoir, *My Life on the Road*, chronicling her itinerant existence as a journalist and activist.

The cocktail dedicated to Steinem is based on the classic "White Lady" cocktail, which has sibling Ladies of different hues (blue, violet, pink, and so forth). This particular Lady is strong and complex.

Anaïs Nin

The Anaïs Nin

1   shot red wine syrup
    (p. 143)
1   shot brandy
½   shot amaretto
1   shot fresh lemon juice
1   shot fresh orange juice
3   shots club soda
    (soda water)
<u>Garnish</u>: sliced apple,
sliced strawberries, and
blueberries

Add red wine syrup, brandy,
amaretto, lemon juice, and
orange juice to a shaker
with ice. Shake vigorously
and strain into a Collins
glass filled with ice. Top
with club soda, garnish,
and serve with a straw.

Anaïs Nin's writing centered the female gaze and
established her as a subversive main character.

Born in France to Cuban parents, she relocated to
New York after her father left her mother. In a house
the family rented when Nin was in her late teens, she
discovered a cache of erotic paperbacks, and wrote in
her diary, "By the time I had read them all, there was
nothing I did not know about sexual exploits … I had my
degree in erotic lore." She dropped out of high school
and, when she was 20, married a wealthy banker.

Early in her career, Nin wasn't successful, but
as a fixture on the literary scene, she used her wealth
to sponsor emerging writers. Famously, she decided
a penniless, unknown, middle-aged author named Henry
Miller was a genius; she had a steamy affair with
him and paid his living expenses for the next decade
while he wrote. Meanwhile, Nin often had to self-
publish her own books—she even worked the printing
press herself. She didn't achieve mainstream success
until age 63, when she published the multivolume
The Diary of Anaïs Nin. Combining detailed accounts
of her life with philosophical ruminations, it made her
a feminist hero. Posthumously, her reputation became
more complicated: first, after it was revealed that
she'd had two husbands, one on each coast, and second,
after early volumes of erotica she'd written were
published. One of those, *Delta of Venus*, was her first
bestseller, eclipsing her earlier work. Her licentious
image was enhanced when "unexpurgated" versions of her
diaries were published that included explicit accounts
of sex with people including Miller.

Today, Nin is remembered as a pioneer—a boundary-
pushing diarist, an inhabitant of the literary avant-
garde, and one of the first to write about sex from
a female perspective. Her cocktail is a love potion
with a flavor profile borrowed from sangria.

Terese Marie Mailhot

The Terese Marie Mailhot**

2   shots Lyre's American
    Malt
½   shot berry syrup
    (p. 142)
3   dashes Angostura
    bitters
Garnish: strawberries
and blueberries

Add ingredients to
a mixing glass with ice.
Stir and strain into
a rocks glass with
a large ice cube.
Garnish with strawberries
and blueberries on
a cocktail pick.

** If you omit the
Angostura bitters, this
cocktail is zero proof.
With the bitters, it has
a low level of alcohol.

Terese Marie Mailhot rejected notions of whom she
should be and what she should write, and in return,
found authenticity and her own voice.

Mailhot grew up on the Seabird Island Indigenous
reserve in British Columbia, Canada. Her mother was a
poet and an activist, and her father was a Coast Salish
artist. Her house was full of books, which she read
prodigiously, including her mother's poetry. As a teen,
she loved Emily Dickinson, and memorized and recited
her poem "I am nobody who are you?"

But Mailhot was often left alone—her mother was
working, and her father, who was violent and abusive,
was away drinking. Mailhot was eventually sent into
foster care, and aged out of the system. She married
as a teen, divorced, and lost custody of her child.
But eventually, as an adult, she got her GED and
attended community college, and in 2016, received
her MFA in fiction from the Institute of American
Indian Arts.

Mailhot said that she had originally been encouraged
to write for a white audience, and her first attempts
were at a novel. But she reversed course and "cut out
all the contrivance," as she told PBS, and the result
was her memoir, *Heart Berries*. Drawing inspiration
from Maggie Nelson's *Bluets*, the book defies traditional
genre conventions and is told as a series of short
essays. It begins with Mailhot having a breakdown in
a mental health facility, and from there details her
story of love, loss, trauma, and healing. It landed on
the *New York Times* bestsellers list, was chosen by Emma
Watson for her book club, and cemented Mailhot's status
as one of the leading figures of the new Native American
Renaissance. She's also an English professor, and since
2017 has taught creative writing at Purdue.

The cocktail dedicated to Mailhot is authentic, and
berry-flavored.

Roxane Gay

The Roxane Gay

2   shots silver tequila
¾   shot strawberry-black
       peppercorn syrup
       (p. 143)
¾   shot fresh lime juice
1   pinch salt
<u>Garnish</u>: dehydrated
lime wheel

Add all ingredients to a
shaker with ice and shake.
Strain into a rocks glass
with ice and garnish.

Multi-genre writer and critic Roxane Gay brings raw honesty, wry humor, and intelligent introspection to any topic she touches. Adept at toggling between high culture and pop culture and as prolific on Twitter as she is on the page, she can be relied upon for frank, unpretentious, and cutting dissections of contemporary society.

Gay grew up in a middle-class Haitian-American family and had a happy childhood, though she was shy and spent much of her time with her head in books. But when she was 12, she went through a life-changing trauma when she was sexually assaulted (a topic she wrote about in her essay "What We Hunger For"). That experience changed her trajectory: she gained large amounts of weight in an attempt to turn her body into a "fortress," and at school, she began writing violent, troubling stories. Seeing her talent, a teacher both helped her find counselling and encouraged her writing, and by her early 20s she was publishing erotica, literary fiction, and nonfiction as she pursued further degrees in academia. She eventually became an English professor, working at both Purdue and Yale, and in 2011, published a short story collection, *Ayiti*, themed around Haiti.

Gay quickly came to prominence in 2014, at age 39, when she published her bestselling essay collection *Bad Feminist*, which explored her ambivalence towards feminist orthodoxy (as well as a wide range of other cultural topics). That same year, she also published her debut novel, *An Untamed State*, which used a fairytale structure for a plot centering on sexual trauma. From that point on, she established herself as a public intellectual, publishing opinion pieces on race, rape culture, and feminism in the *Guardian* and the *New York Times*. She also continued releasing books, including her critically acclaimed 2017 memoir *Hunger*, in which she explores the experience of living in her body and her relationship to food and weight.

The cocktail dedicated to Gay is bold and flavorful, with a kick from black peppercorns.

Joan Didion

The Joan Didion

1	shot bourbon
1	shot mezcal
¾	shot basic simple syrup (p. 142)
½	shot fresh orange juice
½	shot fresh lemon juice

<u>Garnish</u>: orange rind

Add all ingredients to a shaker filled with ice. Shake vigorously, fine strain into a rocks glass with a large ice cube, and garnish.

A prolific novelist, journalist, and screenwriter, Joan Didion's idiosyncratic, melancholy prose and aloof glamour have made her a literary icon since the late 1960s.

Didion grew up in Sacramento, California, and as a child, she was a shy bookworm. By the time she became a teenager, she dedicated herself to studying the famously terse Ernest Hemingway, typing out chapters from his novels to understand their structure. During her final year in college, she won an essay contest for *Vogue* and moved to New York City to claim the prize: a job at the magazine, where she stayed for seven years. She married another writer, John Dunne, and after she published her first novel, the two moved back to California and adopted a daughter, whom they named Quintana Roo.

Didion began writing personally inflected magazine articles about California and cultural upheaval at the tail end of the 1960s, making a name for herself within the New Journalism movement. Several of those essays were published in two collections, *Slouching Towards Bethlehem* and *The White Album*, the latter of which contains her famous essay of the same name and features her best-known quote: "We tell ourselves stories in order to live." She also collaborated with her husband on a number of screenplays, including *The Panic in Needle Park* and *Play It As It Lays*, which was an adaptation of her own novel by the same name.

As Didion grew older, she experienced two great losses: the death of her husband from a heart attack, and the untimely illness and death of Quintana Roo. Probing her grief in her writing, Didion published two memoirs, *The Year of Magical Thinking* and *Blue Nights*; for the former, she won the Pulitzer Prize.

California is the focus of much of her best-known writing; as literary critic Michiko Kakutani said, "California belongs to Joan Didion." Didion's cocktail combines the sunniness of California citrus with the sophistication of bourbon and the subversive, smoky edge of mezcal.

Recipes

SYRUPS

One of the most common cocktail ingredients is simple syrup, and there's no reason to buy it from the store: it's quick and easy to make at home. A basic simple syrup can also be used as a building block for a wide range of flavored syrups. Recipes for simple syrup and a number of flavored syrups that appear in *Buzzworthy* are included here.

Basic Simple Syrup

In a small saucepan, bring ½ cup (120 ml) water and ½ cup (100 g) granulated sugar to a simmer, stirring until the sugar is dissolved. Add any flavorings and allow to cool. Any type of syrup can be stored in the fridge for up to 1 week in a clean, airtight container.

Flavored Simple Syrups

Apricot syrup: In a small saucepan, bring 1 sliced apricot and basic simple syrup to a simmer. Crush apricot to release flavor. Allow to cool, and strain.

Berry syrup: In a small saucepan, bring 2 tbsp (30 g) strawberries, 2 tbsp (30 g) blueberries, and basic simple syrup to a simmer. Allow to cool, and strain.

Blueberry syrup: In a small saucepan, bring ½ cup (65 g) blueberries and basic simple syrup to a simmer. Allow to cool, and strain.

Butterfly pea flower syrup: In a small saucepan, bring 2 tbsp butterfly pea flowers and basic simple syrup to a simmer, and steep until liquid is a dark blue. Strain and allow to cool.

Flower syrup: add a few drops of rose water and a few drops of orange blossom water to basic simple syrup. Bring to a simmer and allow to cool.

Hibiscus syrup: In a small saucepan, simmer basic simple syrup and ½ cup (15 g) dried hibiscus flowers for 5 minutes or until liquid is a deep magenta. Strain and allow to cool.

Juniper-cardamom syrup: In a small saucepan, bring 1 tbsp juniper berries, 1 tbsp green cardamom seeds, and

basic simple syrup to a simmer. Press on juniper and cardamom with the back of a spoon to crush and release flavor. Simmer for 5 minutes, allow to cool, and strain.

Peach syrup: In a small, heavy-bottomed saucepan, simmer 2 small peaches (sliced into small pieces) and basic simple syrup for 5 minutes. Remove from heat, allow to cool, and strain.

Raspberry syrup: In a saucepan, bring ¼ cup (30 g) raspberries and basic simple syrup to a simmer. Simmer for 5 minutes, until syrup is deep red. Strain out raspberries and allow to cool.

Red wine syrup: In a small saucepan, bring ½ cup (120 ml) red wine and ½ cup (100 g) granulated sugar to a simmer until sugar dissolves. Allow to cool.

Spiced plum syrup: In a small saucepan, bring 4 small sliced canned purple plums (aka prune plums), 2 cinnamon sticks, 1 tsp whole cloves, and basic simple syrup to a simmer. Simmer for 5 minutes, allow to cool, and strain, pressing gently on plums with the back of a spoon to release juices.

Strawberry-black peppercorn syrup: In a small saucepan, bring ½ cup (65 g) strawberries, 1 tbsp black peppercorns, and basic simple syrup to a simmer. Allow to cool for 10 to 15 minutes, and strain.

Vanilla syrup: Add 1 tsp vanilla extract to warm basic simple syrup, stir thoroughly, and allow to cool.

Other Syrups

Not all syrups have a simple syrup base; some use other sweeteners, like honey.

Honey syrup: Combine equal parts honey and hot (not boiling) water. Stir until combined.

OTHER INGREDIENTS

Avocado tequila: Combine ½ cup (120 ml) silver tequila and half an avocado in a blender, and purée. Strain through a fine strainer (this may take patience, as the mixture is thick!).

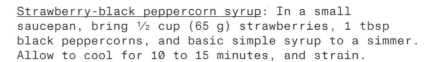

Blood orange ice cubes: Mix 1 shot blood orange juice, ½ shot fresh lemon juice, and ¾ shot basic simple syrup (p. 142). Pour into an ice cube tray and freeze.

Hibiscus-infused white rum: Add 4 shots white rum and 1 handful dried hibiscus flowers to a jar. Allow to sit for 2 to 3 hours, until liquid is a deep magenta.

Lime-mint ice globe: In a mixing glass, combine 1 shot strained fresh lime juice, 1 shot basic simple syrup (p. 142), and 8 mint leaves. Muddle mint leaves. Add 3 shots of water, stir, and pour into an ice globe mold to freeze. Makes one 5-ounce (150 ml) globe.

Raspberry shrub: Add ½ cup (120 ml) white wine vinegar and ½ cup (100 g) granulated sugar to a small saucepan. Bring to a simmer, add 12 to 15 raspberries, and simmer on low for 5 minutes. Strain, and allow to cool.

Spice-infused gin: Place 8 green cardamom pods, 12 cloves, and a 1-inch (2.5-cm) chunk of ginger sliced thinly into a Mason jar. Add ½ cup (120 ml) gin. Gently crush cardamom, cloves, and ginger with a muddler to help release flavors. Cover and allow to sit overnight, and then strain.

Strawberry-and-lime-infused gin: Add 4 sliced strawberries and the rind of one lime (cut into strips) to a container with ½ cup (120 ml) gin. Cover with a lid, allow to sit for 3 to 4 days, and strain. (If there are a lot of tiny bits that can't be strained, filter through a coffee strainer.)

Turmeric-infused vodka: Peel and dice one turmeric root. Place in a container with 1 cup (240 ml) vodka, leave for 24 hours, and strain.

Watermelon rum: In a blender, combine 1 cup (145 g) fresh watermelon and ½ cup (120 ml) white rum. Blend thoroughly and strain through a coffee filter.

TBR List: Suggested Reading

You've made the cocktail, but don't know what to read? This suggested list of books and essays by the authors in *Buzzworthy* will help.

This list is an edited collection of recommended reads that are available in bookstores (or, in some cases, published online) today, not a full bibliography of any writer's work. The selection was very hard to narrow down, and I hope that when you find an author you love, you'll explore all their work.

Writers are listed alphabetically by last name, and their works are ordered by what you should read first.

Chimamanda Ngozi Adichie

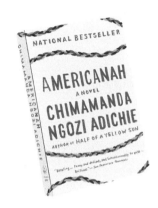

Americanah (novel, 2013)
A novel about the African diasporic experience, *Americanah* centers on a Nigerian woman who becomes famous in the US writing about how Americans view Blackness, and her lover, who lives undocumented in London—and their eventual reunion in Nigeria.

Half of a Yellow Sun (novel, 2006)
Adichie's second novel tells the story of Biafra, a state that seceded from Nigeria and triggered a civil war, and how it affects the lives of three characters.

We Should All Be Feminists (essay, 2014)
This book-length essay arguing for why everyone should embrace feminism was adapted from a TED talk given by Adichie, and was famously sampled by Beyoncé.

Isabel Allende

The House of the Spirits (novel, 1982)
An epic, magical realist novel following four generations of a Chilean family, exploring gender, class, and politics within Chile.

Eva Luna (novel, 1987)
This novel follows the life of an orphan in an unnamed Latin American country (resembling both Chile and Venezuela).

Maya Angelou

I Know Why the Caged Bird Sings (memoir, 1969)
Angelou's memoir of her youth and coming-of-age

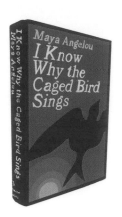

details how her inner strength and love of literature helped her triumph over racism and trauma.

Maya Angelou: The Complete Poetry (poems, 2015)
Released after Angelou's death in 2014, this thick volume brings together a comprehensive collection of her poetry, including the full collection published in the Pulitzer-nominated *Just Give Me a Cool Drink of Water 'fore I Diiie* and the poem she read at the Clinton inauguration, "On the Pulse of Morning."

Jane Austen

Pride and Prejudice (novel, 1813)
Austen's best-known novel is also her most charming, focusing on the witty, intelligent Elizabeth Bennett, one of five sisters of modest means, and her love interest, Mr. Darcy.

Emma (novel, 1815)
A novel about romantic misunderstandings, *Emma* portrays a flawed heroine who is rich, somewhat spoiled, and a bit delusional, and loves to play matchmaker for her friends.

Persuasion (novel, 1818)
Austen's last novel, published posthumously, is also her most complex. The plot centers on Anne Elliott, who, as an "old maid" in her late twenties, has a chance to reconsider an old flame from an engagement she was persuaded to break years earlier.

Sense and Sensibility (novel, 1811)
This is the first novel Austen published, and follows three sisters who experience a change in fortunes and must leave the family estate for a new, more modest home (and romantic adventures).

Eve Babitz

Eve's Hollywood (essays, 1974)
Semi-autobiographical essays steeped in Babitz's decadent, bohemian LA lifestyle.

Sex and Rage: Advice to Young Ladies Eager for a Good Time (novel, 1979)
This may be a novel, but the life of protagonist Jacaranda, an arty, cocktail-swilling LA party girl, mirrors Babitz's own.

Simone de Beauvoir

The Second Sex (nonfiction, 1949)
This groundbreaking feminist philosophical book argues that gender is a cultural construction imposed upon women, paving the way for the women's rights movement of the 1960s and '70s.

Alison Bechdel

Fun Home: A Family Tragicomic (graphic novel, 2006)
Cult-venerated comic artist Bechdel's first
graphic novel, about her coming out as a lesbian
and her relationship with her dad, brought her
mainstream accolades.

Are You My Mother? A Comic Drama (graphic novel, 2012)
After exploring her relationship with her father,
Bechdel turned her attention to her fraught relationship
with her emotionally distant mother.

Octavia E. Butler

Kindred (novel, 1979)
This sci-fi novel about a young Black woman from
the 1970s who travels through time to the Antebellum
south and rescues her white enslaver ancestor to ensure
her own survival remains Butler's most popular.

Bloodchild and Other Stories (short stories, 1995)
Butler's novelette "Bloodchild"—about a colony of humans
and insect-like aliens with whom they coexist—was her
breakthrough, and this collection pairs it with some of
her other short fiction.

Dawn (novel, 1987)
The first book in Butler's Xenogenesis trilogy focuses
on a world where the Earth has been rendered
uninhabitable due to nuclear war, and surviving,
rescued humans interbreed with aliens.

Agatha Christie

And Then There Were None (novel, 1939)
Christie's masterwork is a locked-room mystery where
eight people are invited to an island, then mysteriously
killed one by one.

Murder on the Orient Express (novel, 1934)
One of Christie's Hercule Poirot mysteries, this novel
(which was twice adapted to film) features the Belgian
detective solving a murder on a train between Istanbul
and London. But if you want to start with the first
Poirot book, that would be 1920's *The Mysterious Affair
at Styles*.

A Murder Is Announced (novel, 1950)
If you're new to Miss Marple, you may wish to start with
the novel where she made her debut, 1930's *The Murder
at the Vicarage*. But this one involves an ingenious plot
wherein a future murder is announced in the newspaper,
and when it goes down as predicted, Miss Marple steps in
to solve the case.

Angela Davis

Angela Davis: An Autobiography (memoir, 1974)
Davis' autobiography doesn't just tell her life story as an activist; it also reads as a prison memoir and puts forth an argument for the violence of the state.

Emily Dickinson

The Complete Poems of Emily Dickinson (poems, 1955)
Only a few of Dickinson's boldly original poems were published in her lifetime, but this comprehensive 1955 collection published all 1,775 of them in three volumes. It's still in print today, but is now available in one thick volume.

Joan Didion

Slouching Towards Bethlehem (essays, 1968)
Didion's first collection of nonfiction, parsing her experiences living in California in the 1960s.

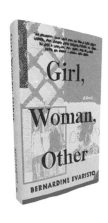

The White Album (essays, 1979)
Didion's second essay collection cemented her ownership of California as a topic, this time ranging into the 1970s. Her influential essay of the same title appears in this book.

The Year of Magical Thinking (memoir, 2005)
A memoir of Didion's year of grief following the death of her husband.

Louise Erdrich

The Night Watchman (novel, 2020)
Inspired by Erdrich's grandfather, this is an epic novel about Ojibwe people fighting against a termination bill in the 1950s.

Love Medicine (novel, 1984)
Erdrich's debut about interconnected Ojibwe families living on reservations in Minnesota and North Dakota.

Bernardine Evaristo

Girl, Woman, Other (novel, 2019)
This novel of poetic fiction portrays the lives of 12 Black British women through interlinking short stories.

Blonde Roots (novel, 2009)
This satirical novel imagines a world in which Africans enslaved white Europeans.

Elena Ferrante

The Neapolitan Quartet (novels, 2011–14)
All four of Ferrante's Neapolitan novels are included here because if you read one, you will read all four.

My Brilliant Friend (2011), *The Story of a New Name* (2012), *Those Who Leave and Those Who Stay* (2013), and *The Story of the Lost Child* (2014) follow friends (and sometimes frenemies) Lenù and Lila from childhood in Naples through to adulthood and old age.

Gillian Flynn

Gone Girl (novel, 2012)
This thriller, famous for its plot twist, subverted stereotypes about murder mysteries and launched a cottage industry of books about complicated women.

Sharp Objects (novel, 2006)
Flynn's debut follows a journalist—another complicated woman—to her hometown to investigate a series of murders.

Roxane Gay

Bad Feminist (essays, 2014)
A series of pop-culture-inflected essays that explore feminism from the perspective of someone who may not observe its orthodoxy.

Hunger: A Memoir of (My) Body (memoir, 2017)
A candid memoir of Gay's relationship with weight and food.

Amanda Gorman

Call Us What We Carry (poems, 2021)
A collection of poems of hope and healing in the wake of the global pandemic. Includes the famous poem Gorman recited at the Biden inauguration, "The Hill We Climb."

Sheila Heti

How Should a Person Be? A Novel from Life (novel, 2010)
Heti's first book to capture widespread attention is autofiction involving artists and writers (and a main character named Sheila) searching for the best way to live.

Motherhood (novel, 2018)
In another volume of autofiction, a character named Sheila weighs one of the biggest questions to face women: whether or not to procreate.

S. E. Hinton

The Outsiders (novel, 1967)
This novel about warring teenage gangs—the Greasers and the Socs—established YA fiction as a genre.

bell hooks

Ain't I a Woman? Black Women and Feminism (nonfiction, 1981)
A feminist work examining the intersecting forces impacting Black women.

All About Love: New Visions (nonfiction, 2000)
A critique of how we view love in contemporary society that aims to change how we think about it, and how we interact with each other.

Zora Neale Hurston

Their Eyes Were Watching God (novel, 1937)
A Harlem Renaissance classic about a woman's search for love and identity.

Barracoon: The Story of the Last "Black Cargo" (nonfiction, 2018)
Written in 1931 and published posthumously, *Barracoon* is a detailed account of slavery told from Hurston's 1927 interviews with Cudjo Lewis, the last man brought from Africa to America on a slave ship.

Rupi Kaur

Milk and Honey (poems, 2014)
Originally self-published, Kaur's illustrated debut volume of "Instapoetry," on the topics of love, loss, trauma, and healing, connects with a broad audience with its simple, emotional verse.

The Sun and Her Flowers (poems, 2017)
Kaur's second popular book of poems focuses on growth, healing, love, loss, and femininity, and proved her staying power within poetry.

Jhumpa Lahiri

Interpreter of Maladies (short stories, 1999)
Lahiri's Pulitzer-winning debut ties together nine short stories about Indians and Indian Americans navigating dislocation and cultural belonging.

The Namesake (novel, 2003)
Lahiri's debut novel exploring similar themes to *Interpreter of Maladies* is the coming-of-age story of an Indian American child named after Nikolai Gogol.

In Other Words (memoir, 2016)
A memoir of how Lahiri moved to Italy and learned to express herself in Italian.

Ursula K. Le Guin

A Wizard of Earthsea (novel, 1968)
The first of Le Guin's series of six high fantasy novels set on an oceanic world named Earthsea follows a young wizard as he learns to control his power.

The Left Hand of Darkness (novel, 1969)
The fourth book in Le Guin's Hainish Cycle of novels and short stories explores a world where gender doesn't exist.

The Dispossessed (novel, 1974)
Another Hainish Cycle novel, this book centers on a physicist who aims to heal the rift between his utopian-anarchist home planet and its capitalist neighboring planet.

Harper Lee

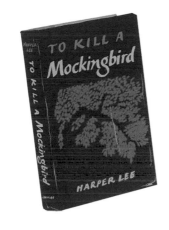

To Kill a Mockingbird (novel, 1960)
Lee's classic novel about racial injustice, centered on a precocious white girl in the South, Scout, and her lawyer father, Atticus Finch, who defends a Black man accused of raping a white woman.

Min Jin Lee

Pachinko (novel, 2017)
A sprawling, historical novel about Korean Japanese people and how they have persevered under oppression.

Free Food for Millionaires (novel, 2007)
The story of a Korean American woman trying to make it on Wall Street and afford a glamorous, high-society life.

Audre Lorde

Coal (poetry, 1976)
Lorde's first volume of poetry with a major publisher explores her identity as a "Black, lesbian, mother, warrior, poet."

Sister Outsider: Essays and Speeches (essays, 1984)
This collection of essays takes an intersectional view on oppression and inspired a generation of feminists.

Carmen Maria Machado

Her Body and Other Parties (short stories, 2017)
In this collection Machado uses genre trappings (sci-fi, horror, and fantasy) to spin fantastical, twisted and funny tales about womanhood.

In the Dream House (memoir, 2019)
This wildly creative memoir examines Machado's relationship with an abusive ex-girlfriend through different tropes, fluidly changing tone with each short chapter.

Terese Marie Mailhot

Heart Berries: A Memoir (2018)
This unconventional memoir is a series of short essays connecting Mailhot's Indigenous identity, her trauma and healing, and her relationships with her family, children, and romantic partner.

Toni Morrison

Beloved (novel, 1987)
Morrison's best-known novel tells the story of Sethe, a formerly enslaved woman who is haunted by the ghost of her dead daughter.

Song of Solomon (novel, 1977)
Morrison's third novel is one of her most acclaimed, and follows the life of Macon "Milkman" Dead III from birth in Michigan to adulthood and his quest for hidden treasure and his family's roots in the American South.

Sula (novel, 1973)
Set in a poor Black neighborhood in Ohio called the Bottom, *Sula* follows two girls, Sula and Nel, and the different paths their lives take.

The Bluest Eye (novel, 1970)
Morrison's first novel confronts white beauty standards with the story of a Black girl, regarded by those around her as ugly, who yearns for blue eyes.

Sayaka Murata

Convenience Store Woman (novel, first published in English 2018)
The first of Japanese author Murata's books to be translated into English, this novel's protagonist is a woman who rejects the expectations of society and finds her purpose in working at a convenience store.

Celeste Ng

Little Fires Everywhere (novel, 2017)
A complex family drama exploring transracial adoption, class, and racism in a privileged community in Ohio.

Everything I Never Told You (novel, 2014)
Ng's debut is an emotionally complex portrait of a mixed-race Chinese American family whose daughter drowns in a lake.

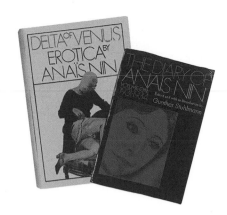

Anaïs Nin

The Diary of Anaïs Nin (memoir, multiple volumes, 1966–)
The many diary volumes documenting Nin's life—some "unexpurgated," including the raciest parts of it—made her a literary star.

Delta of Venus (short stories, 1977)
The erotic short stories in this collection were written in the 1940s by Nin for a private collector, for a dollar a page.

Joyce Carol Oates

"Where Are You Going, Where Have You Been?"
(short story, 1966)
A short story about a teenage girl sucked into the orbit of a malevolent, mysterious man, Arnold Friend. Inspired by the 1960s serial killer Charles Schmid.

them (novel, 1969)
A tragic novel following the struggles of a working-class, dysfunctional family in Detroit over three decades.

We Were the Mulvaneys (novel, 1996)
The story of a seemingly perfect, status-conscious family whose lives fall apart after their teen daughter is raped.

Blonde (novel, 2000)
A fictionalized story about the inner life of Marilyn Monroe.

Mary Oliver

American Primitive (poems, 1983)
Oliver's Pulitzer-winning collection contains poems about nature, love, and wildness, and contains her famous poem "In Blackwater Woods."

New and Selected Poems: Volume One (1992)
Winner of a National Book Award, this collection includes new poems as well as selected poems from Oliver's eight earlier books, including the oft-quoted "The Summer Day" (originally published in 1990's *House of Light*) and "Wild Geese" (originally published in 1986's *Dream Work*).

Torrey Peters

Detransition, Baby (novel, 2021)
A complex, funny, genuine novel about a man (detransitioned after living as a transgender woman) who is potentially having a baby with his cis-woman boss-slash-lover and needs the involvement of his ex, a trans woman, to make it all work.

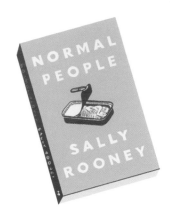

Sally Rooney

Normal People (novel, 2018)
This steamy story of an on-again, off-again romance follows the popular Connell and the awkward Marianne from high school through university in Ireland, examining their intense connection and their traumas.

Conversations with Friends (novel, 2017)
Rooney's debut explores the connection between two best friends in their twenties and a married couple in their thirties—and the inevitable, sexually fraught affair between the husband, Nick, and the emotionally repressed Frances.

Beautiful World, Where Are You (novel, 2021)
Best friends Alice (a successful novelist) and Eileen (a less successful editor) and their intellectual correspondence about the state of the world threads through this book about their relationships with Felix and Simon, and their tenuous hold on adulthood.

Arundhati Roy

The God of Small Things (novel, 1997)
Inspired by Roy's life, this is the tragic story of a family in India whose lives are torn apart by a love affair across castes.

The Ministry of Utmost Happiness (novel, 2017)
Roy explores dark events that have shaped post-Partition India through the interconnected lives of characters from across the continent.

Marjane Satrapi

Persepolis: The Story of a Childhood (graphic novel, first published in English 2003)
This groundbreaking black-and-white graphic novel tells the story of Satrapi's childhood during the Islamic Revolution in Iran as she watches religious extremism transform the life she knew.

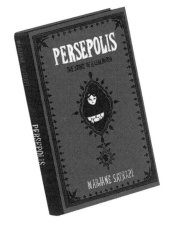

Persepolis: The Story of a Return (graphic novel, first published in English 2004)
Picking up where the last volume left off, 14-year-old Satrapi flees for a new life in Vienna, where she must make her way as a teenager far from friends and family. Eventually, she returns to Iran, where she finds love and belonging, but faces tough questions about her future.

Mary Shelley

Frankenstein; or, The Modern Prometheus (novel, 1818)
The first example of science fiction, Shelley's
Frankenstein examines the morally complicated results
of a scientist reanimating a corpse.

Patti Smith

Just Kids (memoir, 2010)
Smith proved her literary mettle and broke hearts
with this memoir documenting her relationship with
photographer Robert Mapplethorpe against the backdrop
of late 1960s and '70s New York.

Zadie Smith

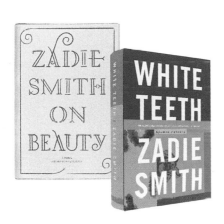

White Teeth (novel, 2000)
Smith's wildly popular debut *White Teeth* tells
interlinked stories of two North London families
over decades.

On Beauty (novel, 2005)
An homage to *Howards End* by E. M. Forster, this novel
centers on a mixed-race family in the United States and
the liberal/conservative culture war as it stood in the
early aughts.

Swing Time (novel, 2016)
A sprawling story about tap dance, pop stardom, and
the coming-of-age of two mixed-race girls in London.

Feel Free: Essays (2018)
Smith is a virtuoso essayist as well as novelist, and in
this collection she bends her mind towards subjects as
diverse as global warming, Facebook, and Justin Bieber.

Susan Sontag

"Notes on 'Camp'" (essay, 1964)
This essay, which defined a till-that-moment underground
sensibility of artifice and exaggeration celebrated
by the queer community, launched Sontag into fame and
remains her best-known piece of writing.

Against Interpretation (essays, 1966)
This collection of essays and criticism includes the
titular essay, which argues against reading meaning into
art in favor of appreciating it on aesthetic grounds.

Gloria Steinem

Outrageous Acts and Everyday Rebellions (essays, 1983)
A collection of the essays Steinem became famous for
publishing in various magazines, including her exposé
"I Was a Playboy Bunny," and "If Men Could Menstruate,"
a satirical essay about, well, what the title says.

My Life on the Road (memoir, 2015)
Steinem has lived a remarkable life in the public eye, and this memoir follows her experiences as a journalist and activist.

Amy Tan

The Joy Luck Club (novel, 1989)
Tan's most successful book focuses on a Chinese American woman, June, who takes her mother's place in her mah-jongg club after she passes away—and learns about her mother's generation and her ancestral home. A novel about mother–daughter relationships, it also includes forays into the relationships of the other mah-jongg players and their daughters.

The Kitchen God's Wife (novel, 1991)
Inspired by Tan's mother's life, this novel involves mother–daughter relationships, family secrets, and immigration to America post-World War II.

The Bonesetter's Daughter (novel, 2001)
This tender novel centers on a Chinese-American daughter caring for her aging mother with dementia, and her discovery of the truth about her mother's life in China.

Donna Tartt

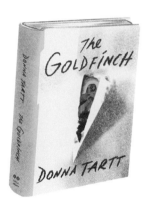

The Secret History (novel, 1992)
Tartt's debut novel centers on an insular group of Classics students at a liberal arts college, revealing how they murdered one of their friends, and how the murder affects their lives.

The Goldfinch (novel, 2013)
An expansive (771-page!) novel following the survivor of a terrorist attack on an art museum and the ripple effects of his decision, in the aftermath of the attack, to steal a painting called *The Goldfinch*.

Jia Tolentino

Trick Mirror: Reflections on Self-Delusion (essays, 2019)
A collection centering on the ways modern culture—including scams, self-optimization, and the internet—shapes the way we live now.

Lindy West

Shrill: Notes from a Loud Woman (essays, 2016)
Both funny and earnest, West's mix of memoir and polemic launched a new wave of body-positive feminists—and was later adapted into a popular television show.

Virginia Woolf

Mrs Dalloway (novel, 1925)
A day in the life of a high society woman in postwar London, and one of the most famous stream-of-consciousness novels.

To the Lighthouse (novel, 1927)
Using third-person omniscient narration, with multiple viewpoints, this philosophical novel focuses on a family's visits to the Isle of Skye between 1910 and 1920.

Orlando: A Biography (novel, 1928)
Inspired by the life of the writer Vita Sackville-West, *Orlando* tells the story of a poet who lives for centuries and changes gender from male to female.

"A Room of One's Own" (essay, 1929)
Woolf's famous essay explores women's social and economic freedom and how it affects their ability to create.

About the Author and Illustrator

Jennifer Croll

Jennifer Croll is the author of several books about cocktails and culture, including *Free The Tipple*, *Dressed to Swill*, *Art Boozel*, *Bad Girls of Fashion*, and *Fashion That Changed the World*. Earlier in her career, she spent several years as a book reviewer for an alt weekly. During the daytime, she's a book editor, and at night, she makes cocktails—and is thrilled to combine her two loves in *Buzzworthy*.

Rachelle Baker

Rachelle Baker is a *New York Times* bestselling illustrator and artist from Detroit, Michigan. She has illustrated *Shirley Chisholm Is a Verb* by Veronica Chambers, *Stamped (for Kids): Racism, Antiracism, and You* by Jason Reynolds and Ibram X. Kendi, and *The Motherlode: 100+ Women Who Made Hip-Hop* by Clover Hope. When she's not drawing, she is yelling about comics, dancing, and thinking about drawing.

Acknowledgments

Jennifer Croll

Utmost gratitude to Ali Gitlow for believing in *Buzzworthy*, acquiring it, and helping make it great. Katherine Latshaw at Folio Literary Management, your wise feedback was essential in making this book a reality. Martha Jay, thank you for carefully watching over my words, and Nina Jua Klein, much gratitude for your beautiful, literary design. Rachelle Baker, I love how you captured these writers' personalities. And thank you to the many brilliant people at Prestel who help make these books a success (Andrew, Ryn, and everyone else—I appreciate it!).

For my family and friends, your support means so much to me. Dad: I appreciate your effort to learn to make cocktails. I am in debt to Doretta Lau for thoughtful advice along the way, and thankful to Michael Mann for understanding when I'm in the cocktail bunker. To my colleagues at Greystone, I am grateful for your excitement and cheerleading for my alter ego.

Thank you, most of all, to the authors I've profiled in this book—I hope that I've helped a few readers find your work.

Rachelle Baker

Mom and Jacob, thanks for always listening to me when I feel unheard and overwhelmed, and for the pep talks. To Linda Camacho for supporting and advocating for me, you are simply the best. To my iPad Pro for keeping it together and staying alive through all of the cracks and tumbles, I love you, cracked screen and all. Big shout out to my dog, Doobie, for forcing me to take lots of breaks in between work to give you snacks and take you on walks. You'll never read this because you are a dog, but you are the MVP (occasionally).

© Prestel Verlag, Munich · London · New York, 2023
A member of Penguin Random House Verlagsgruppe GmbH
Neumarkter Strasse 28 · 81673 Munich

© for the text by Jennifer Croll, 2023
© for the illustrations by Rachelle Baker, 2023

Library of Congress Control Number: 2022944124

A CIP catalogue record for this book is available from
the British Library.

Editorial direction: Ali Gitlow
Copyediting and proofreading: Martha Jay
Design and layout: Nina Jua Klein Studio
Production management: Luisa Klose
Separations: Reproline Mediateam, Munich
Printing and binding: Livonia Print, Riga
Paper: Magno Natural

Penguin Random House Verlagsgruppe FSC® N001967

Printed in Latvia

ISBN 978-3-7913-8916-5

www.prestel.com